Magnetic Nortl

# SEX
# &GOD

## Linda McLean

**First performance at Platform, Glasgow,
on 27 September 2012**

# SEX & GOD

## Linda McLean

## Cast

| | |
|---|---|
| Jane | **Ashley Smith** |
| Lizzie | **Lesley Hart** |
| Sally | **Louise Ludgate** |
| Fiona | **Natalie Wallace** |

| | |
|---|---|
| Director | **Nicholas Bone** |
| Designer | **Claire Halleran** |
| Lighting designer | **Simon Wilkinson** |
| Sound designer | **Kim Moore** |
| Voice director | **Ros Steen** |

| | |
|---|---|
| Production Manager | **Mickey Graham** |
| Stage Manager | **Emily Bull** |
| Technical Manager | **Laura Hawkins** |
| Wardrobe Supervisor | **Katy Lonsdale** |

| | |
|---|---|
| Producers | **Verity Leigh & Dani Rae** |
| Press & Marketing | **Dani Rae** |
| Illustration & Designer | **Anna Parker** |
| | **for fogbank.co.uk** |

Produced in association with **Platform**

*Sex & God* was commissioned by **Magnetic North**

# Magnetic North°

Magnetic North is a theatre company based in Edinburgh, Scotland. It was formed in 1999 by theatre and opera director Nicholas Bone to create and develop new work.

We work with actors, playwrights, designers and composers to produce theatre that is stylish, articulate and individual.

The main focus of our development work is Rough Mix, which is an opportunity for theatre-makers to collaborate with other practitioners, try out new ideas and introduce them to an audience.

We place the writer at the centre of the play-making process, whether the play is a new commission or an existing text. We encourage playwrights to experiment with form, structure, content and narrative.

Previous work includes *Pass the Spoon* by David Fennessy, David Shrigley and Nicholas Bone (co-production with Southbank Centre, London); *Wild Life* by Pamela Carter (co-production with Cumbernauld Theatre); *Walden* by Henry David Thoreau, adapted by Nicholas Bone; *After Mary Rose* by D.Jones; *Word for Word* by Linda McLean; *My Old Man* and *The Dream Train* by Tom McGrath; *Braziliana*, an interactive website by Ronan O'Donnell, Scott Fleming and Steven Davismoon; and *Swan Song*, a film written by Joern Utkilen.

Future plans include *SOS*, a new play by Clare Duffy; a tour of *Pass the Spoon* and a new performance and visual-art event inspired by walking, called *A Walk on the Edge of the World*.

Magnetic North Theatre Productions Ltd
*email*: mail@magneticnorth.org.uk
*web*: www.magneticnorth.org.uk
Registered charity SC029351

# Biographies

**Nicholas Bone (director)** is Artistic Director of Magnetic North and has directed all the company's work, including: *Pass the Spoon, Wild Life, Walden, After Mary Rose, My Old Man, Word for Word* and *The Dream Train*. Other theatre includes: *Mad Forest* (Gateway); *Skunk Hour* (lookOUT); *Safe Delivery* (Jumping Genes); *Territory of the Heart* (Theatr y Byd); *La Ronde* (ATC) and *Six Characters in Search of an Author* (RSAMD). Opera includes: *Happy Story*, also co-librettist (Scottish Opera); *Carmen, Lucia di Lammermoor* (Haddo House); *Paradise Moscow, Hansel and Gretel, L'enfant et les sortilèges* (RWCMD); *Peter Grimes* (Co-Opera Kent); *Così fan tutte* (Music Theatre Kernow). Nicholas specialises in the facilitation of cross-art-form collaboration and leads Magnetic North's creative-development programme Rough Mix.

**Emily Bull (stage manager)** is a freelance stage manager based in Edinburgh. She has a Masters degree in Contemporary Theatre Practice and studied at the Royal Welsh College of Music & Drama. She has worked on productions including: *The Wizard of Oz* (Royal & Derngate, Northampton); *All My Sons, Peter Pan, The Long Road* (Curve, Leicester); and *Happy Days* (Crucible, Sheffield). She has also been involved with projects and events for the National Theatre, London, HighTide Festival, Queer Up North Festival and Mayor's Thames Festival. She has worked on pieces for the Edinburgh Festival Fringe (*Dust* at the New Town Theatre, *The Prime of Miss Jean Brodie* at Assembly Hall).

Most recently Emily has been involved with the Scottish Youth Theatre's summer festival, as well as a number of projects at the Royal Conservatoire of Scotland.

**Mickey Graham (production manager)** has worked with many Scottish companies including: NVA, National Theatre of Scotland, Janice Parker Projects, Vanishing Point, Vox Motus, MacRobert Arts Centre, Dundee Rep, The Gaelic Arts Agency, Stellar Quines, Mull Theatre, Catherine Wheels, Benchtours, Traverse Theatre, Wee Stories, Boilerhouse and Edinburgh International Festival.

He has also worked for Walk the Plank (Turku European City of Culture 2011), the Bush Theatre (London), and the Lyric Theatre (Belfast).

**Claire Halleran (designer)** is a graduate of Glasgow School of Art, and Master of Fine Art, Queen Margaret University. Claire is delighted to be working with Magnetic North again. Her first design with the company was *After Mary Rose.*

Other design credits include: *What Happened Is This, Naked Neighbour* (Never Did Nothing); *Paperbelle* (Frozen Charlotte); *Mr Snow, The Night Before Christmas, Rudolf, The Littlest Christmas Tree* (macrobert); *Forgotten Forest, Luvhart, First Light, My House* (Starcatchers); *Ignite* (YDance/Smallpetitklein); *Reasons to Dance, Allotment* (National Theatre of Scotland); *The Sun, The Moon and a Boy Called River* (Wee Stories); *Visualise, Crime Scene Investigations, Dr Clot's Blood Curdling Adventure, Wee Wonder World* (Edinburgh International Science Festival/Abu Dhabi International Science Festival); *The Pilgrimage, Ballerina Ballroom – Cinema of Dreams* (Mark Cousins/Tilda Swinton); *Beneath You, Mouth of Silence, Brazil 12 – Scotland 0* (Birds of Paradise); *Otter Pie* (Fish & Game); *The Art of Swimming* (Playgroup).

**Lesley Hart (LIZZIE)** trained at RSAMD. Theatre includes: *27* (National Theatre of Scotland); *Lady M* (Theatre Jezebel, Tron); *The Silence of Bees* (Arches) *Slice* (Gilded Balloon/Òran Mór), *Sins of the Father* (Rowan Tree); *Futureproof* (Traverse/Dundee Rep); *What Love Is* (Òran Mór/Dundee Rep); *Wild Life* (Magnetic North); *The Uncertainty Files* (Paines Plough/Òran Mór); *The Silver Darlings* (APA); *The Cherry Orchard* (Lyceum); *Autobahn* (Theatre Jezebel); *The Dirt Under the Carpet* (Òran Mór/Paines Plough); *Long Time Dead, Strawberries in January* (Paines Plough/Traverse); *Tiny Dynamite* (Paines Plough/Frantic Assembly); *Elizabeth Gordon Quinn* (National Theatre of Scotland); *Shimmer, Outlying Islands, Among Unbroken Hearts, Shetland Saga* (Traverse); *Nightingale and Chase, A Midsummer Night's Dream, The Twits* (Citizens).

Film and television includes: *Bob Servant, Independent* (BBC4); *Taggart* (STV); *Casualty, Invisible Kids* (BBC1); *Fast Romance, The Way* (Ickleflix).

**Laura Hawkins (technical manager)** graduated with a degree in Lighting Design from Rose Bruford College. After working as a Technical Manager Laura now works as a freelance Lighting Designer, Technician and Production Manager. Recent credits include: Room 2 Manoeuvre, Plutôt la Vie, Edinburgh International Fashion Festival, Errol White Company, Theatre Cryptic, CackBlabbath Presents, Traverse Theatre, Pitlochry Festival Theatre and Dundee Rep's *Sunshine on Leith*. Laura also designs and makes jewellery under the banner of Little Red Star www.littleredstar.etsy.com

**Verity Leigh (producer)** is a freelance producer based in Edinburgh. She has also worked with Forced Entertainment, Quarantine and Wee Stories.

**Katy Lonsdale (wardrobe supervisor)** studied Performance Costume at Edinburgh College of Art, graduating in 2003. Since then she has worked as a freelance Costume Designer/Maker/Supervisor working on various theatre productions, television, student films and dance. She works regularly for National Theatre of Scotland and Yorkshire based Mikron Theatre Company. Her most recent project was a large costume sculpture featured in Alnwick Gardens.

**Louise Ludgate (SALLY)** trained at Glasgow's RSAMD. Her theatre work includes: *Home*, *Realism*, *The House of Bernada Alba* (National Theatre of Scotland); *Mainstream*, *Casanova*, *Lament* (Suspect Culture); *The Adoption Papers*, *Straw Girl* (Manchester Royal Exchange); *Greta* (Traverse); *Iron* (Traverse/Royal Court); *Little Otik* (Vanishing Point /NTS); *Home Hinderance* (Vanishing Point /Fire Exit); *Sub Rosa* (Citizens/Fire Exit); *The Lion, the Witch and the Wardrobe* (Citizens); *The Crucible*, *The Devils*, *The Wedding* (The Arches); *Balgay Hill* (Dundee Rep); *Jeff Koons* (ATC); *Slice* (Gilded Balloon/Òran Mór); *Dig* (Paines Plough/Òran Mór); *Shattered Head* (Traverse/Òran Mór); *Resurrection*, *Moonwalking*, *Out on the Wing*, *The Date*, *Wired* (Òran Mór); *The Hanging Tree* (lookOUT).

Film and television includes: *Spooks*, *River City*, *Freedom*, *Kissing, Tickling and Being Bored*, *Sea of Souls*, *Glasgow Kiss* (BBC); *Taggart*, *High Times* (SMG); *Night People* (New Foundland films); *The Elemental* (Northlight). Extensive radio work for the BBC.

**Linda McLean (playwright)** grew up in Glasgow where she studied and trained as a teacher. She travelled teaching English as a foreign language in Europe, America, Africa and Scandinavia before she wrote plays. Linda is chairwoman of the Playwrights' Studio Scotland and has worked for the British Council in Mexico City, Teluca and Bogota. She regularly works in schools and colleges, encouraging new writers to find their own voices. In 2009 she delivered the keynote speech to the Playwrights' Guild of Canada. From 2010–2011 Linda was Creative Fellow at Edinburgh University's Institute of Advanced Studies in Humanities. Linda's play *Any Given Day* received its US premiere at the Magic Theatre, San Francisco, in spring 2012.

**Kim Moore (sound designer)** studied music at Glasgow University. As well as composing, she performs in improvised work and used to play with the band Zoey Van Goey. With the band she recorded two albums and composed music for *Dolls* with National Theatre of Scotland.

Kim is interested in collaborative process. She has worked with various visual artists to create sound-installation work and performances for young people. These include: a bike-powered outdoor sound sculpture for GIANT, a musical resonating bed for the Tramway and an immersive installation, of hidden sounds explored in torch light for The City Halls.

Kim also works in theatre and dance, composing scores for live ensemble and recorded soundtrack. Earlier this year she was a composer for Scottish Music Centre's 24 hour composer's marathon, composing for laptop and cello, and she also took part in the Rough Mix residency with Magnetic North. www.kimikomoore.com

**Dani Rae (producer/press & marketing)** is a freelance producer, dramaturg and consultant. She has worked with and for some of the UK's leading arts agencies and theatre companies including: Edinburgh Festival Fringe Society, Imaginate, Starcatchers, Gill Robertson, Wee Stories Theatre, Reeling & Writhing, Royal Lyceum, Errol White Company and Plutôt la Vie. Recently Dani worked with Berlin-based contemporary circus producers Circle of Eleven (supported by FST's Producer's Bursary) as booker and PR for their multi-award-winning production *LEO*. She also produces for Wolfgang Hoffmann's Aurora Nova Productions managing Nassim Soleimanpour's *White Rabbit Red Rabbit* and for Summerhall, Edinburgh's newest creative hub for the arts. www.danirae.co.uk.

**Ashley Smith (JANE)** trained at RSAMD. Recent theatre credits include: *27* (National Theatre of Scotland); *Futureproof* (Traverse); *Lady M* (Theatre Jezebel); *Don Giovanni, Bunnies, An Incident at the Border* (Òran Mór); *Mother Courage* (Birds of Paradise); *The Snow Queen* (Royal Lyceum); *Magic Spaghetti* (LicketySpit); *Sense* (Frozen Charlotte); *Pobby and Dingan, Hansel and Gretel* (Catherine Wheels); *Peer Gynt* (Dundee Rep/NTS); *Baby Baby* (Perissology/Stellar Quines); *Nasty, Brutish and Short* (Traverse/NTS); *365* (NTS); *Liar* (TAG). Radio includes: *The Seagull, Side Effects* (Bona Broadcasting); *McBeth's McPets* (BBC Radio Scotland).

**Ros Steen (voice director)** For Magnetic North: *Wild Life, Walden, Word for Word*.

Other theatre work includes: *Macbeth, The Missing, Beautiful Burnout, Black Watch, Mary Queen of Scots Got Her Head Chopped Off* (National Theatre of Scotland); seasons for the Traverse Theatre, Citizens Theatre, Royal Lyceum and Dundee Rep as well as productions for the Edinburgh International Festival, Tron Theatre, West Yorkshire Playhouse, His Majesty's Aberdeen (including national tours), Perth Theatre, Òran Mór, Paines Plough, Vanishing Point, Borderline, Visible Fictions, Stellar Quines, lookOUT, untitled and TAG. Films include: *I Love Luci, Greyfriars Bobby, Gregory's Two Girls, Stella Does Tricks*.

Television includes: *Sea of Souls, Rockface, 2000 Acres of Skye, Monarch of the Glen, Hamish Macbeth* and *Looking After Jojo*. Radio includes: *The Other One, Gondwanaland, The Meek* and *Look Back in Anger* for BBC Radio 4.

She is currently Professor of Voice at the Royal Conservatoire of Scotland.

**Natalie Wallace (FIONA)** trained at Drama Centre London. She recently finished the Graduate Scheme at Dundee Rep where she played Shelby in *Steel Magnolias,* Pinkie in *Baby Baby,* Tixylix in *Cinderella,* Serena in *Futureproof* (co-production with the Traverse) and Megan in *Forfeit* (co-production with Òran Mór).

Other theatrical credits include the reopening of the Royal Shakespeare Theatre with the RSC. Television and film credits include: *The List* (Winner Best Short Film BAFTA Cymru 2010); *Blue Line* (Flyboy Films) and *Wham Bam Strawberry Jam* (CBBC).

**Simon Wilkinson (lighting designer)** is an associate artist of Magnetic North, having designed lighting for *Pass the Spoon, Wild Life* and *After Mary Rose*. For Vox Motus his designs include: the award-winning *Slick, Bright Black, The Not-So-Fatal-Death of Grandpa Fredo* and their recent co-production with the Royal Lyceum Theatre Company, *The Infamous Brothers Davenport*.

Other recent theatre work includes: *The Static* (ThickSkin); *Skewered Snails* (Iron Oxide); *Roman Bridge, Truant* (National Theatre of Scotland); *Zorro, The Hunted* (Visible Fictions); *PUSH* (Curious Seed); *Antigone* (Lung Ha's); *After the End, Top Dog/Under Dog* (Citizens Theatre); *Encourage the Others* (Almeida); *Honk!* (Royal & Derngate) and the 2010 season for Pitlochry Festival Theatre.

Simon's lighting has won a Guinness World Record, caused reports of an alien invasion, and attracted tens of thousands of people to a windswept highland forest.

# SEX & GOD

## Linda McLean

*For Nicholas Bone*

2

## Characters

*Four adult women, whose stories take place at different times in the twentieth century and in this order:*

JANE
LIZZIE
SALLY
FIONA

*and* HANNAH

## Note on the Text

*A double forward slash (//) indicates characters saying the same thing at the same time.*

*A single forward slash (/) indicates interrupted speech.*

*The Bible references are from Psalms 83, 85, 86, 101 and 102.*

*Hannah was the childless woman in the book of Samuel, her name means favour/grace/beauty.*

*'Coulter's Candy' was a jingle for a sweet, written by Robert Coltard in the mid-nineteenth century.*

## Thanks

With grateful thanks to Ros Steen, Linda McLaughlin, Molly Innes, Julia Taudevin and Carmen Pieraccini.

*This text went to press before the end of rehearsals and so may differ slightly from the play as performed.*

JANE        Ali Bali Ali Bali Bee
            Sittin on your mammy's knee
            Greetin for a wee bawbee
            To buy some Coulter's Candy

LIZZIE      How come you've never got any

SALLY       not my

FIONA       i don't

LIZZIE      money

SALLY       fault

FIONA       care
            i don't need you
            i'm doing it anyway

JANE        // with what?

LIZZIE      // with what?

SALLY       // with what?

JANE        she'll do it
            she'll do it
            you know her
            i know her, he says
            i know her and she won't go against me, He says
            it's not how she's been brought up
            brought up?
            brought up? i say
            what do you know about how she's been brought
            up?

            *An invisible hand strikes* JANE *and* SALLY.

            // aaa

SALLY       // aaa

LIZZIE      oh

FIONA      why do you stay?

JANE       …

FIONA      // eh?

SALLY      // eh?

           eh? he says
           is this the silent treatment?
           are we getting the silent treatment?
           talk

JANE       // …

SALLY      // …

FIONA      // …

LIZZIE     i can't speak
           words fly out my mouth
           air
           empty air
           i forget what they might have meant
           i look at the
           place
           they might have been
           some place between my nose
           that's funny
           between my nose and
           his
           nearly like a kiss
           that light
           but but but
           but the thing that
           the tie between
           that ties the
           what i want to say
           and
           is
           i
           forget, he says
           forget

SALLY      i'm not well is all

| | |
|---|---|
| FIONA | let me see<br>let me see |
| SALLY | really<br>it was just a bad night |
| FIONA | look at me<br>look at<br>aw naw<br>naw<br>where else? |
| SALLY | no<br>nowhere |
| FIONA | // why do you stay? |
| JANE | // why do you stay? |
| SALLY | it doesn't matter where i go<br>he'll find me |
| JANE | // he doesn't like to be<br>// crossed |
| SALLY | // he doesn't like to be<br>// crossed |
| LIZZIE | // cross my heart and hope to die<br>fall down dead if i tell a lie |
| FIONA | there are places<br>places you can go |
| SALLY | and who'll look after your sister? |
| LIZZIE | and her<br>my wee broken angel<br>who'll take care of her? |
| JANE | don't speak about it now<br>we'll speak about it later<br>when it's longer ago<br>and we're better |
| LIZZIE | but |
| FIONA | but |
| SALLY | but |

JANE        but nothing

LIZZIE      don't you listen to them Robert says
            they don't love you the way i do
            i know how he loves me
            he loves me with his eyes and his hands and his
            all-over body
            i feel it
            i feel him tremble
            aye he trembles just when he shouldn't
            just when he wants to be something else
            tough
            hard
            and instead his arms
            the muscles in his arms flutter
            he never fails me, never
            and i see the flutter and tremble
            but i'm not afraid that he's not strong enough
            so when he says don't you listen to them
            i only feel his breath on my hair and on my neck
            and i'm not listening to anything else nothing
            no words / come close to this listening in my
            // skin.

JANE        as if she's the only one who ever felt the // skin of
            a man's body
            and his need
            and wanted it on her
            and around her
            and in her

LIZZIE      Ali Bali Ali Bali Bee
            When you grow up you'll go to sea

FIONA       i'm leaving
            i'm going to
            Away
            i'm going to far-away places
            foreign places
            countries i can't even pronounce
            i'm going to make my own way
            i'm going to be

LIZZIE      Makin pennies fur yur daddy an me

SALLY        to apply for a job i say
             what job?
             you don't need a job, he says
             oh just a job, you know
             in a hospital
             no i don't know, he says
             i'm the one with the job
             i'm the one with the job i hate
             i stay at the job i hate because of you and them
             they need a roof
             and food and clothes
             he says
             we don't need a wife with a job

LIZZIE       To buy some Coulter's Candy

JANE         one of the cleaning jobs starts at five
             i'm up at four
             you can waken at four no trouble
             four is a good time
             five or six is bad
             you waken up at five or six and your second sleep
             hangs on you all day
             but something about four is different
             i call it the wide // hour

FIONA        // our university is shit
             i don't know anybody
             there are black holes in the day that i don't know
             how to fill
             i'm supposed to go to the library
             but this library is full of exams
             this library is against life
             and every book that i love
             i love books
             and i love reading
             the way they make you believe in
             what they make you believe in
             i can tell you where i was
             i can tell you what i was
             what i needed rescued from by every book i ever
             read
             the page numbers are my minutes

days
weeks
months
years

LIZZIE        you sit there my wee angel
sit there now
Mammy has to go out
Mammy has to get us tea
you know you don't like the street
there are goats and giants and goblins in the street
aye goats
me-eh me-eh
and you're too wee
so you stay here
promise me
promise me

SALLY        we could have extras i say
like
like
what, he says
and i say

LIZZIE        here's a bit of sugar for you darling

SALLY        i could have // extra

FIONA        // sex
with boys
or men
well maybe men later
but i'm definitely going to have sex
on tables
in baths
and i will have candles
and lingerie
and a balcony bra
on a balcony
in a hot country
and be hot
and
and cool

all at once
i'll have things i don't even know / yet

JANE        i work for a lady over the river
a gentlemanly kind of lady
she's very kind
she's the very kind of lady my mother used to talk
about
my mother was a lady's maid
but only because she was a clever girl
before that she was just a kitchen maid like me
she carried pails
she did
and pee'd in the grass
she did
my mother said that everything she was
everything we were
the things that made us better
were all thanks to that lady
that lady was a benny // factor

LIZZIE      the // factor turned up today
somebody wasn't doing their job, Robert says
somebody is always supposed to be on the look-out
the factor cannot be walking down this road and
we not know about it
the factor can not come to this door and us be in
the factor will run us // out of here

FIONA       i've run // out of money
i remember a pound that i have in the bank
account they made me open when i enrolled
and so i go in there and i say
i want to have that pound please
i'm already thinking that with that pound i can buy
some out-of-date vegetables
i like vegetables, even soft ones
and i live with Polish girls
who'll get me some chicken wings for next to
nothing
really cheap cheap
because they know how to shop at the butcher's

just when he's closing
it's even better than sell-by shopping
and they always have some potatoes left
but the bank has a rule
it has a rule
whether you're hungry or not
that you have to leave one pound in the account
unless you want to close it
and if you close it you have to pay money to
reopen it
and my money goes in there tomorrow
so i can't close it
and even if i do close it i can't have the pound
today
it's my pound
and i was banking on that pound
but i can't get my pound
and i can't go back and just hang around waiting
for some leftover potatoes like a down and out

SALLY      you promised me, i say
you swore you'd stop
you said you wouldn't any more
you're supposed to take me to work
he looks at me
he raises his eyebrows
look at you, he says, swaying
look at you // standing there

JANE       // standing there in your bare feet
carrying a pail of You Know What
not even your own You Know What
the Mister and Missus You Know What
so you don't even want to breathe over it
and the sky is tipping itself on your head
and the groom's boy from the stables
the one with the brown eyes and wide shoulders
steps in your path
well then you're only as fine as your pride
and you're only as fine as you wear it
and the finest worn pride is as light as the lace on
the faerie flag

he won't see it in your clothes or in your work
and you can't say it in words
but when he looks at you and a hundred things fly
through his head
he has to take account of it
and he has to respect it

LIZZIE i'm very sorry sir but if you could come back
tomorrow, i say to the factor's man
i'm sure my husband will be here to settle our
account
when Robert comes home he picks me up and
swings me round and says
where do you get it, darlin?
all your la-di-da ways
you were born in a byre but you're as fine as a lady
and he twirls me
i'm a butterfly
or a sycamore seed
flying through the air
but he didn't see the factor's man
and he isn't there when the factor's man grabs me

FIONA and i get very low when i'm hungry and i'm
hungry now
hungry and ashamed
i know if i stood on the street and asked somebody
for money i could present them with a compelling
case for giving me some
i know i could
and i would promise to send them the money
when i got it
i *would* send them the money when i got it
i'm a woman of my word
girl of my word
and i see a number of people who look nice enough
but i have // pride

JANE // pride is what separates us from the pigs

SALLY pig

LIZZIE pig

FIONA      and i walk straight off the pavement
           i don't see the road
           or the car
           and it hits me
           and i'm thrown up onto the bonnet
           i don't think i even say oh or ah
           i just slide off and keep walking
           and the guy in the car he gets out and runs after me
           he's shaking
           and he stops me and says
           are you all right? are you all right?
           and then
           you just walked straight in front of me
           there was nothing i could do
           and i don't answer him
           and he keeps on walking beside me because i
           haven't stopped and then he stands in front of me
           so i can't go on
           and i move to the side
           all this with nothing more than the pound in my
           mind
           i don't think i felt the car
           not then
           but i realise he won't go away until i speak to him
           and tell him it isn't his fault
           it isn't your fault, i say
           and then
           i'm fine, really
           and he settles a bit
           really, i'm fine, i say
           and he goes back to his car and gets in and drives
           past me
           and as he's driving past he shouts
           YOU SHOULD LOOK WHERE YOU'RE
           GOING
           all red-faced and angry
           and revs up the engine and squeals off
           and i'm standing there // looking at nothing

SALLY      // looking at me like that for?
           i have a job

it's important to me
it's
people need me to turn up on time
to shovel their shit, he says
you like shovelling shit, he says
and i see he's more and less drunk than i thought
his head has switched
and i've said too much

JANE i can't have you here
i'm surprised you came
and lucky for you your father's not in
take what He'd give you
you made that bed, lady
you made that bed and you'll have to lie on it

FIONA oh god, oh god oh god oh god uh uh uh uh
uhhhhhhhhhhhhhhhhhhhhhhhhhhhhhhhhhhhhhhhhhhhh

*Post-orgasmic laughter.*

why did nobody // tell me?

LIZZIE // tell me your name, he says
first him then her
what's your name?
do you know your name?
can you tell us your name?
i
i
you forget? they say
i know something
i know

SALLY // he loves me

FIONA // he loves me

LIZZIE // he loves me

JANE // he loves me

LIZZIE too much
he loves me too often
every time i look down there's another one
growing

i look at him and say
how many?
can you remember how many there've been?
he looks at me
God he loves me
if there wasn't already one growing in me he'd
make another one now
it's a gift and a curse all at the same time
how many?
how many??

FIONA   seven at the last count
not that i'm keeping count but someone asked me
and i had to go through them in order
one
two
three
four
who was after that?

LIZZIE  of course i know my name
my name is

FIONA   five oh yes
and then six
six is
six has
six can take you to a place where the breath goes
in and out of your body so fast and so light that
you think you've found a way to breathe
underwater

SALLY   (*Gasping for breath.*)
stop
urgggggg
stop
please
gurggggg – (*Underwater drowning sound.*)

JANE    gurgggg – (*Husband drowning in fluid on the lungs.*)

LIZZIE  gurgggg – (*Drowning in opiate.*)

FIONA    but six doesn't know what he wants
         he tells a good story

LIZZIE   you're my princess, he says
         and the bairns love to hear him tell it
         i was walking down the street
         minding my own business, he says
         and they all stop and settle down
         all the clambering and scuffling and squabbling
         flies out the window
         and there she was, he says
         walking, she'll call it
         but i say she was floating
         she was a faerie
         and i don't know what brought her here but she
         certainly didn't have the hang of the pavement
         because i looked at her feet and they were moving
         all right
         i mean to the ordinary passer-by it might look as if
         she was actually taking steps
         but not to me
         no
         I've seen faeries before
         and they all share one thing in common

JANE     you don't think straight

SALLY    you need help

JANE     you'll perish, girl
         if you can't toughen up
         you'll not be spared when

LIZZIE   their feet don't actually touch the ground
         thing is
         no one thinks to look at a faerie's feet because
         they're mesmerised by their eyes
         their rare green eyes

JANE     the Devil comes looking for liars and thieves

FIONA    // no

SALLY    // no

LIZZIE     // no

JANE       // no

SALLY      // run

LIZZIE     // run
           wrap everything you can in a shirt and run

SALLY      for my life
           i've seen it before
           that look in his eye when he's seeing something
           other than me
           something so bad he can't bear the torment of it
           has to annihilate it
           batter it flat
           squeeze the breath out of it
           hurl it with all of his might
           dash it against the wall
           i fall

LIZZIE     i can't go any further
           a great tightening around my middle has brought
           me to my knees
           go on go on
           Robert looks back at me
           go on, i say
           i'll be right there
           get them away
           and he bundles them together as if he were a
           sheepdog
           and hurries them off down a back street
           // please

FIONA      // please, i whisper

SALLY      // please, i whisper
           please
           don't
           // don't

FIONA      // don't leave me
           don't leave me?
           i can't believe i'm saying it

i'm desperate
i'm nothing
i've reduced myself to nothing

// less than nothing

JANE        // less than nothing

LIZZIE      // less than nothing

SALLY       it's me
            me
            i see a flicker

LIZZIE      of pity when the factor's men see my belly and i
            can't get up
            // get up

SALLY       // get up

FIONA       // get up

JANE        // get up

SALLY       he says
            i say, i love you
            another flick and he's back to what he was as if the
            very sound of the words was the trigger

LIZZIE      and one of them kicks me
            right there in the street while people carry bags
            past me
            with fruit and

FIONA       he runs away

SALLY       // please

JANE        // please

FIONA       // please

LIZZIE      // please

            *All four protect themselves from something.*

            ah

FIONA       ah

JANE      ah

SALLY     ah

          FIONA, SALLY *and* LIZZIE *fall to the ground.*
          FIONA, LIZZIE *and* JANE *recover before*
          SALLY.

JANE      don't ever come back here looking for money

FIONA     because i won't be here next time you just feel like
          it
          please

SALLY     please

          .

          .

          .

LIZZIE    stop pushing, says the woman at the bare place
          they've taken me to
          stop pushing
          i'm not pushing
          it's my baby, she's pushing her own way out of me
          you can't have a baby in here
          no babies allowed
          take her outside
          there's a woman three doors down
          she'll take you in for a shilling
          i haven't got a shilling
          it's not my business, she says
          take her outside
          they lift me up but i can't walk so they drag me to
          the front door
          i think they're going to push me down the stairs
          my baby
          my baby
          i say
          and they put two arms under my arms and carry
          me down
          my baby

JANE        was put in me without my permission
            but i could not speak of it
            // could not

FIONA       // could have been a girl or a boy
            i've no way of knowing and it was too soon to tell,
            they said
            but they never used the word baby
            which i was glad of
            i didn't let it form in my mind
            what i need is

JANE        abstinence

FIONA       contraception

SALLY       fixed

LIZZIE      i drag myself up to the door and i knock on it
            i knock on it again
            a child opens the door
            i don't have a shilling, i say
            Mammy, he shouts, there's a woman at the door
            and she says she hasn't a shilling
            the pushing is all push now
            i've no need to do anything but give in

JANE        or it's endless babies and debt and the poor's
            house

FIONA       abortion

JANE        i can't

FIONA       or give it away and think no more of it

SALLY       if you can

JANE        who will it go to?

FIONA       somebody with money and a job and a roof
            you can be sure of that

JANE        do you promise?

LIZZIE      and then she's born
            right there on the street

FIONA      just hand her over

LIZZIE      it's a dirty street
there's mud and mess and dog mess and fag ends
and things i don't know covered in a layer of black
dust or muck
but i've got
i'm filled with so much
i feel so
strong
such strength
let them come now
let them touch me now
i have the love of the world in me
around me
light
i'm filled with light
and she's lying in my mess
right there on the pavement
surrounded by dirt
and everywhere is dirt
even me
i'm dirty
but She is filled with blessed light
as none of my other babies have been
as if
as if
Christ is in her
shining out of her
and i want to bow to her
kneel
so i kneel
and she holds out her arms
pick me up, she says
and i pick her up
you know me, she says
i know her
i'm sorry, i tell her
they say babies are blind but she looks right at me
and the light from her runs into me

FIONA       give her up

JANE        a girl

SALLY       another girl

JANE        don't give her a name, they say
            it'll only make it harder

LIZZIE      her name is Hannah

JANE         i whisper it to myself

SALLY       don't you want to look at her? they ask me

JANE        you mustn't even think a name

LIZZIE      Hannah

SALLY       isn't she lovely, they say?

LIZZIE      the woman of the house comes to the door and
            tries to take her from me

SALLY       // no

JANE        // no

LIZZIE      // no

JANE        she pinches my arm so hard i scream

SALLY       // no

JANE        // no

            and the other one puts her arm round my neck and
            shoulders
            and they take her

LIZZIE      just until you get up, she says

JANE        i don't trust them

FIONA       it's dead

SALLY       i don't want to look at her

JANE        don't take her
            please don't take her

LIZZIE     the woman has a good face so i give her my angel
           and i stand up
           she looks at the baby
           and she looks at me
           and she says
           there's something strange about this baby
           and i look at my baby and i look at the woman and
           i say
           i know
           she's an angel
           and she sits me down on a chair covered with
           newspapers
           and gives the baby back to me
           she smiles at me and i smile at her
           i've never felt so happy

JANE       sad

FIONA      empty

SALLY      trapped

           i ask the surgeon if he can stop me from having
           any more and he pats my arm and says 'very wise'
           and i make a decision

           // never again.

JANE       // never again.

FIONA      // never again.

LIZZIE     // never again.

           .

           .

           .

LIZZIE     What you need is a pick-me-up, he says

JANE       a good strong cuppa

SALLY      a sense of humour

FIONA      a whisky

i've never liked the taste of it but i say okay
a whisky and Coke then
are you mad? he says
you'll spoil the // whisky

JANE          // whisky is the Devil's work

SALLY         his face is swollen, puffy, blotchy

LIZZIE        but he is calm and smiling
not agitated
try this he says
try one of these

FIONA         i smell it for a long time
i love the smell
the bog
bark
brackish water
sun and wind
and the feeling you get when you've walked long
enough on the sprung earth and

SALLY         i wonder if he was always ugly
if i had only imagined the beauty of him

LIZZIE        is it safe? i ask him
it's electric, he says
come to the window
come here to the window

FIONA         and the sky is not so far away
and the ground is soft beneath your feet
a warm sun is on your neck
your shoulders drop
and the breath spreads into your body and fills you
with / peace

JANE          a nice cup of tea at the League and plain home-
cooked food
there's always something of the Almighty on the
table
a verse
a tract

LIZZIE    it's magic
          the city is lit up
          one day, he says
          one day it'll be ours
          we're hungry, i say
          not for much longer, he says
          he says he's got a job on top of his other job
          one underground
          the other in the dark
          but we're hungry now, i say
          take this then
          here
          i'll put it between my lips and we'll take it
          together

JANE      For I have eaten ashes like bread, and mingled my
          drink with weeping,
          Because of thine indignation and thy wrath:
          For thou hast lifted me up, and cast me down

FIONA     and need meets want

SALLY     i feel sick
          i can't let him see i feel sick
          i want him to stop
          i say

LIZZIE    i'm so tired

FIONA     our tongues are serpents

SALLY     stop

FIONA     don't stop

LIZZIE    this'll make you feel better, he says

SALLY     he revolts me

JANE      I will behave myself wisely in a perfect way

FIONA     we're turning ourselves inside out

SALLY     he stops and looks at me
          his eyebrow raised
          don't show it, i tell myself

|  | don't let him see<br>// don't |
|---|---|
| FIONA | // don't stop don't stop don't stop don't stop |
| LIZZIE | and suddenly i am filled with joy |
| SALLY | he hurts me<br>i don't stop him<br>he hurts me more<br>but now it's different |
| JANE | Wilt thou be angry with us for ever?<br>Wilt thou draw out thine anger to all generations? |
| LIZZIE | do you feel it? he asks |
| FIONA | oh god |
| SALLY | i hate him |
| LIZZIE | i feel it |
| JANE | In the day of my trouble I will call upon thee |
| FIONA | god<br>oh god |
| JANE | For thou WILT answer me |
| LIZZIE | oh heaven<br>is it heaven? |
| SALLY | he closes his eyes |
| FIONA | we close our eyes |
| LIZZIE | i don't know if i'm him or me |
| JANE | As the fire burneth a wood |
| LIZZIE | we're alight |
| FIONA | i was dead |
| SALLY | i am nothing |
| JANE | And as the flame setteth the mountains on fire |
| FIONA | we're lost |

| | |
|---|---|
| LIZZIE | we're flying |
| SALLY | he has consumed me |
| JANE | I watch, and am as a sparrow alone upon the house top |
| LIZZIE | out of breath |
| SALLY | in a rhythm all his own |
| FIONA | listening to every rise and fall |
| LIZZIE | i want |
| FIONA | i want |
| SALLY | i want |
| LIZZIE | i |
| FIONA | him |
| SALLY | to |
| LIZZIE | need |
| FIONA | i |
| LIZZIE | this |
| SALLY | i<br>// need |
| FIONA | // need |
| SALLY | i wish |
| JANE | Truth shall spring out of the earth |
| FIONA | oh god oh god oh god oh god |
| LIZZIE | is good<br>is good<br>is good |
| SALLY | i wish he |
| FIONA | oh |

LIZZIE      i
            wish
            we

FIONA       oooh

JANE        And righteousness shall look down from Heaven

SALLY       i wish he was

LIZZIE      we need
            we need
            we need

FIONA       ah
            ah
            ah
            aaahhhhhhhh

LIZZIE      more
            more

FIONA       oh god
            why did nobody tell me?

JANE        Fill their faces with shame; that they may seek thy
            name

SALLY       // i wish

LIZZIE      // i wish

FIONA       // i wish

# BOOOOOM

SALLY       he was dead.

LIZZIE      i always felt like this.

FIONA       i'd met you first.

JANE        Lord.

            .

            .

            .

JANE      There are things that will be required of you after
we marry, he says
is that right, i say
he's a groom's man and he can hardly write
is that right?
well you needn't think i'll be letting you poke
your thing inside me whenever you want, says i
i am a decent girl
in that case there are other things that will be
required of you after we marry, he says
he's a groom's man and he can hardly write
you'd better get to know this little man
Todger, he calls him
when Todger is up, Todger has to run
and you'll have to hold on to him
and keep up with him
or what else are we marrying for?

LIZZIE    i can't do without him

SALLY    he lifts me up
as if i'm made of nothing
the black of his eyes grows wide and i'm

FIONA    gone, solid gone

SALLY    just a girl

LIZZIE    who can't say no

JANE      Todger is often up
and i hold on to him
and keep up with him
but i can't get used to the custard at the end
and then people start asking me if everything is all
right
In That Field
oh well, they say, we thought we might have cause
for celebration by now
and they're not talking to me
they're talking to my middle part
oh
ohhh
oh yes, // i say

SALLY       // i say
            everything is fine
            fine and dandy

JANE        i'm sorry God hasn't seen fit to bless you, the
            minister says
            right after church
            right in the line
            what, i say?
            what?
            Blessed are the children who come unto me, he
            says

            // no, i say

FIONA       // no, i say
            marry you?

JANE        God loves me
            God knows me and he loves me
            and i am good in God's eyes

FIONA       you must be joking, i say
            he looks as if i've hit him
            what?

LIZZIE      the good in my heart
            the good in my spirit
            the good in my body
            is all one with him

FIONA       i'm poor
            i come from
            poor
            i have nothing
            i have only my self
            i can work
            i can learn
            i can
            i can be with you
            i can stay
            but i can't be
            i can't be
            caught in that

| | |
|---|---|
| SALLY | solemn state<br>not to be entered into lightly<br>or without consideration<br>each of you will bind themselves over to the other<br>in the sight of witnesses<br>in the eyes of the law<br>and you will pledge to be faithful, loyal and true<br>till |
| SALLY | // death separates you |
| FIONA | // death separates you |
| LIZZIE | // death separates you |
| JANE | // death separates you |
| SALLY | from that kind of thinking<br>there will be no more from me |
| LIZZIE | babies |
| SALLY | no more |
| LIZZIE | babies |
| FIONA | no more |
| LIZZIE | babies |
| SALLY | no more |
| LIZZIE | babies |
| FIONA | babies |
| JANE | would Todger like to come home? |
| LIZZIE | endless babies<br>years and years of |
| FIONA | babies, it turns out<br>aren't as easy to come by as they once were<br>they require planning<br>and timing<br>and knowledge of temperature<br>and anatomy |

JANE     pushing up in the place where things come down
and it's sore
do people get used to it?
or is something wrong with me?

SALLY     wear this, he says, and holds up a red corset with
suspenders
put this on
i take it and turn to go
no
here, he says
put it on here
in front of me
no, i say
not a big no
not a strong no
more of a
oh no

FIONA     yes now, i say
you have to come home and do it now
that's what the strip says
it was you who wanted this
you said you'd do this
you'd see it through
unless you don't actually want to // make a baby

SALLY     // make it worth watching, he says
please don't make me
i'm awkward
or ugly
or stupid
i don't know what to do with a corset
i'm clutching it as if it's the thing that's saving me
from having to do what he says
or do you want me to do it for you? he says
i can't think my way through that one
which would be worse?
he decides by himself and takes everything i'm
wearing off
he isn't gentle

i'm back at school being humiliated in front of
everyone
i'm clutching my breasts and crossing my knees
but he's enjoying it
i can see he's going to carry on with it
take my clothes off now, he says

FIONA    it doesn't work like that
i have to want to, he says
you know?
don't be silly, i say
here
look
touch this

SALLY    // i don't want to

JANE    // i don't want to

LIZZIE    i think there must be something wrong with me
because i know what will happen
but i have no mind of my own
i only have to say no and he'll stop
i know he will
but my mind belongs to some other time
my mind was somewhere else before it came to me
it's much stronger than i am and when it's made
itself up
i can't go against it
i'm already losing the fight with my body
my body is one half of something and he is the
other
it's the same for him
he's not like some men i see who're half of nothing
whose eyes are so easily caught and strayed
he doesn't see further than me

SALLY    but he's not really seeing me
he's seeing maybe the red
he makes me do up the buttons of the corset
he's rubbing himself against my bum while i try to
do up a million of the smallest buttons in the world
i'm not doing very well

FIONA     i just can't
          it isn't working for me, he says
          come on, come on, i say
          we can do this
          it's making a baby for Christ's sake
          people do it all the time

JANE      morning noon and night, it seems to me
          seems to me he only has to smell me near him
          and wham
          i'm lying on my back
          how long can it take?

FIONA     it doesn't tell you that
          just
          when you're hot you're hot

SALLY     and now the nylons, he says
          bend over and put on the nylons
          i bend
          slowly, he says
          he slaps my bum
          and then he slaps it harder

FIONA     i need to be taken by surprise, he says

SALLY     i get halfway up
          stay there, he says
          stay there
          half-bent over
          half-standing up
          off balance
          he grips my flesh really hard
          i'm damned if i'll cry
          i wobble a few steps so I can grab on to the arms
          of the chair

LIZZIE    there's a whole world of babies in me
          if i could have a baby every month how many
          would that be?

FIONA     boo, i say

JANE      i don't bleed this month

FIONA     surprise surprise

SALLY     i hear him trying to hang on to it
          trying to make it stop coming
          but he can't

FIONA     Boo

JANE      and i'm as regular as a clock

SALLY     uuuuuuuuhhhh, he says through his teeth

FIONA     don't be ridiculous

LIZZIE    hundreds for sure
          running all over me
          scrabbling at me
          needing things

FIONA     i can't keep doing this, he says
          i'm not going to make it

SALLY     and pushes me away
          i fall against the chair

FIONA     BOO

LIZZIE    what was i thinking?
          where was my mind
          what have i done?

FIONA     i don't want this to be my life, he says
          and closes the door gently behind him

JANE      i'm having a baby
          he's neither up nor down
          aye
          so i'll not be having Todger in there interfering
          with it, i say

SALLY     lose some weight, he says
          you're getting fat

JANE      that's what you think, he says

FIONA     boo

LIZZIE      she loves that
            she puts her hands over her eyes and says Look
            for me, Ma
            and i have to kid on she isn't there
            where are you?

SALLY       // boo

JANE        // boo

LIZZIE      // boo

FIONA       // boo

LIZZIE      where are you?

            .

            .

            .

FIONA       Nothing prepares me for the shock of Nairobi
            minutes after i arrive the rains come
            i think I'm going to be washed away
            and then just as suddenly they stop
            and as they dry the smell of jasmine and
            bougainvillea wafts its way around me
            the trees are
            the animals are
            the people are
            the roads are
            the food is

            // everything is

SALLY       // everything is

FIONA       // different

SALLY       // different now

JANE        i put her in a basket outside the kitchen door
            cook says as long as i do the work and she doesn't
            cry
            she'll put up with it
            but if the missus finds out i'm done for

FIONA    there are servants in the house who pick through
         everything we throw away
         and they bow to me
         and even lower to the Kikuyu

LIZZIE   peekaboo
         i see you

FIONA    in Bogota there are people dying on the side of the
         road
         a man who looks as if he's sleeping is standing
         against the wall near the restaurant where we're
         eating
         a girl i'm with wraps up everyone's leftovers and
         takes them outside to him
         his eyelids are so heavy they don't open properly
         when she gives him the food she tells him to eat it
         a little at a time
         and chew very slowly

JANE     she has a fever
         she's so wee
         she's burning

LIZZIE   no
         no
         no

JANE     we can't have children here, they say
         don't you have someone who can look after it?

SALLY    i hide the application under my coat
         but when i let myself in i see he isn't there
         i run into the girls' room to see if they're all right
         they're fine
         they're fast asleep

FIONA    Mexicans know how to dance
         it's a very different beat, made up of five beats not
         four so your hips are always slightly off to the side
         it's like trying to keep up with someone who
         walks too fast

JANE     we have nowhere to go

> we have nothing of our own
> we came here with them
> they give us everything
> house, food, work, money
> little enough of that
> but enough
> what else can we do?

FIONA    in Teotihuacan a woman pulls the sharp tip off a
maguey plant and it has long fibrous threads
attached to it
which she uses to sew skins together
and a man shows me how to crush tiny cochineal
grubs to make a brilliant red dye

SALLY    i go downstairs and knock quietly on the door
she's got a baby
i don't want to waken him
but it's early enough and my knock is soft enough

JANE    i've got a friend who went to the town
she wasn't going to be anybody's servant, she said

FIONA    *vad gora du?* they ask me in Sweden

SALLY    she comes to the door
she's dyed her hair blonde
it must have been just today or last night because i
saw her yesterday and her hair was red then
bold i thought when i saw it that red
but she mustn't have liked it
today she's blonde
and she's a bit unsteady as she opens the door
when she sees it's me she opens it wide and giggles

FIONA    *nista na pravom putu*, they tell me in Croatia

JANE    there's only dirty work to be had in the town, i say
behind factory gates
under the ground
below stairs
servants
in darkness
it's no worse than we are here, he says

FIONA       *trinkst du bier?*

LIZZIE      not
            no
            not a drop
            not a simple single singo drop, i say
            are you hungry?
            you lambs must be hungry
            did you think i'd forgotten you?
            tut tut
            // shhh

SALLY       // shhh
            she puts her finger to her mouth but misses and it
            bumps into her nose
            she laughs
            come on in, she says
            may as well bring the whole family
            i'm backing away
            i don't want to go in
            and i've forgotten what i came for
            briefly
            and then i see Him
            peeking round the door as if he's five years old
            and he's just been caught with his fingers in the
            sweetie tin

JANE        is there no other way?

FIONA       *sono triste in Italia*

JANE        he looks at the child i'm holding

SALLY       // and i know

FIONA       // and i know

JANE        // and i know

LIZZIE      what they think
            but no
            my babies love me
            don't you my lambs?
            see

you see
it's you they're scared of
with all your banging down the door
and uniforms
they're scared you're going to take them away
see
see
and it was just this once

JANE i'll never do it
i'll never let them take another one
there isn't a day goes by that i don't think of / her

SALLY what goes on while i'm not here
what if?

FIONA i don't want to be on my own any more?

SALLY there's an accident?
while he's downstairs
with her
drunk
and the kids are asleep

JANE // no

FIONA // no

LIZZIE my wee angel does a rolly polly
they're playing rolly polly on the floor
she's so fast

FIONA i get off a bus in Haifa
there's a woman who looks pregnant behind me
i stop to let her go before me
but she signals her stomach and waves me on

SALLY what if there's a fire?

LIZZIE please
i beg you

FIONA the air around me draws in a sucking breath
every fibre of my body lines up
and

SALLY     then where would we be?

FIONA     booooooooooooooooooooooooom
          the bus explodes
          i'm // lost

JANE      // lost in this city
          i'm lost

FIONA     and every fibre of my body is in disarray

LIZZIE    it was just the one time

SALLY     he says

FIONA     can we go back to how we were before?

JANE      // there's no going back to that

SALLY     // there's no going back to that

LIZZIE    a wee party
          my neighbour came in with a little bottle of

SALLY     hate the smell of

JANE      on his breath the taste of

SALLY     stay and have a wee drink, she says

LIZZIE    and i just stepped out to get some chips
          see
          here they are
          and i hold them out
          but the paper is wet and soft in the middle
          and the chips fall on the floor
          my babies all run to pick them up
          as if it's a game
          and the woman in the dark coat says
          lift them
          lift them
          they're starving

SALLY     i turn on my heels and say
          no thank you
          i won't come in
          and walk back up the stairs

                    no thank you
                    i won't come in
                    i hear her say as she shuts the door

FIONA               and i am suddenly alone

JANE                i know i'll never see that place again
                    or the hills
                    or the burn
                    or the fresh air
                    i know all about the black air in the town

LIZZIE              you've no right
                    you've no right
                    they're mine
                    you can't take them
                    come back here
                    come back here
                    they're screaming
                    but she's making them go

SALLY               i get halfway up the stairs and miss a step
                    i put out my hand to steady myself against the
                    wall
                    and the application falls onto the stairs

LIZZIE              // aaaaaaaa

FIONA               // aaaaaaaa

SALLY               // aaaaaaaa

JANE                // aaaaaaaaa

                    what am i doing here?

FIONA               what am i doing here?

SALLY               what am i doing here?

LIZZIE              what am i doing here?

                    .

                    .

                    .

JANE          At least we'll never be hungry as long as you're
              working in a kitchen, he says
              Big Hammy makes us open our coats before we
              go home
              but he'd never feel my chest
              not with my man being the coachman
              and him being strong and Hammy being a bit soft
              and it's only one or two chicken legs, the odd
              piece of meat
              meat's scarce and always accounted for
              i'm not above scraping leftovers off the plates
              as long as they don't look chewed
              and even then

FIONA         it's not something i've felt the need for since i was
              a child
              and the velvet curtain of the confessional
              and the smell of the incense
              and the flickering candles mesmerised me
              but it was an impulse
              a pretty white church in Italy
              on a hot day
              with the sun scorching my neck
              and a blinding headache driving me to shade

LIZZIE        they've taken my children, i tell him
              he's so far above me i can hardly see him
              for good reason, He says
              no, i say
              they're mine
              given to you by the Good Lord
              entrusted to you
              His most precious of tasks
              and you have shown yourself to be
              undeserving

SALLY         superior vena cava
              inferior vena cava
              right atrium

LIZZIE        i'm in a temporary state of difficulties, i say to him
              speak up, He says
              what is the woman saying?

SALLY          right ventricle
               AV tricuspid valve
               chordae tendineae

FIONA          and it's in Latin

LIZZIE         // i don't understand

SALLY          // i don't understand

FIONA          // i don't understand

JANE           // i don't understand

               what they're saying half the time
               the people in this town have a terrible way of
               spitting their words
               as if they've a cough they never got over
               and the sounds all run together

SALLY          pulmonary trunk
               pulmonary semilunar valve
               pulmonary artery
               pulmonary vein
               left atrium

LIZZIE         but then i see one of the PCs
               and he sees me
               the look on his face says sorry
               he reads a list of things

FIONA          mater
               i can make that out
               Maria
               and there's a gasp as a woman falls over
               a woman near the front
               and then another
               and more gasping and the priests motion the
               people to sit but look confused

LIZZIE         theft he says
               i never stole anything
               bread from the baker's front stall, he reads
               sausages off the butcher counter
               money from strangers
               no

not me
it's somebody else
they've got me mixed up with somebody else
it wasn't me, i call up
Be Quiet

SALLY    left ventricle
AV bicuspid valve
chordae tendineae
papillary muscle

JANE    i see them looking at me
because
i don't speak like them
even though we're all in the same building
sharing the same stairs
and lavatories
and wash house
i am not like them
i get up at four and go to work
while my girls are asleep
and i come home when he goes off on his shift
and my girls can read
and write
and they can speak the King's English

LIZZIE    no, i say again
you've got me mixed up with someone else
these are not charges against you, Him up there
says
these are the charges against your children
no
my children are good children
Be Quiet
be quiet or mlum mlum mlum mlum mlum

FIONA    and it becomes obvious that something is
happening
people are crowding around the statue of the
Virgin
it's impossible to see without moving forward
i want to move forward

                    i want to be one with the thing that's happening
                    and i don't care if it doesn't make sense
                    my thinking mind is elsewhere

LIZZIE          mlum mlum mlum mlum

SALLY           ascending aorta
                    aortic semilunar valve
                    aortic arch
                    thoracic aorta

JANE            i teach my eldest to cook
                    i leave everything ready and as soon as her father
                    gets in the door
                    she takes his jacket and his hat and salutes him
                    he taught her to salute
                    and she likes the gold braid on his uniform
                    the wee one gets his slippers
                    while the eldest puts the pot on the range and
                    cooks his tea
                    scones, if we've the sugar

LIZZIE          mlum mlum mlum mlum

SALLY           The heart is the muscular pump of the
                    cardiovascular system.
                    It contains four cavities, or chambers; two on the
                    right side (pulmonary heart), two on the left
                    (systemic heart)

LIZZIE          muum muum muum muum

FIONA           as if we're all breathing and moving together
                    and finally i see it
                    i see it and i fall down with the rest of them
                    it's impossible not to
                    we're all one heart
                    we're all one mind
                    we're all one / body

SALLY           Blood is pumped into the right and left ventricles
                    simultaneously through the atrioventricular
                    orifices, guarded by the tricuspid valve on the
                    right and the mitral valve on the left

FIONA     there are milk-coloured tears running down the
          Virgin's face
          and we know it's true
          we know it isn't a trick
          the statue is crying
          she's crying for us

LIZZIE    muum muum muum muum muum

JANE      it doesn't matter how hard we work
          there's no let-up
          every day the same
          apart from Sunday
          i thank God for Sundays

FIONA     // dear god

LIZZIE    // dear God

SALLY     // dear god

JANE      // dear God

# BOOOOOM

SALLY     // i'll never understand this.

LIZZIE    // i'll never understand this.

JANE      // i'll never understand this.

FIONA     // i'll never understand this.

          .

          .

          .

FIONA     When you wish on a star you find the right words,
          don't you?
          it seems somehow very important to get the words
          exactly right
          or your wish might go astray
          or be altered
          you say, i want to be a princess and have a coach
          and horses and beautiful dresses like Cinderella

or i wish it was Christmas every day
or i wish Grandpa wouldn't die
or something like that
everybody wishes their own thing in their own way
but this
this prayer in a church in Italy is a physical thing
i don't know if i can tell you the words even now
a single rush of a wish that explodes out of me
before it can find the words to speak itself
my heart skips a beat and then lurches in an
entirely unfamiliar manner
and i know

LIZZIE      i've been asleep for a long time
no
not asleep
like a sleep
but with no rest

JANE      he's sat on his chair and he says i don't think i can
get up today

SALLY      he gets smaller and smaller
with every day i work
and study
i work harder
and sit exams
i work more
and study more
i pass more exams
he gets littler and littler

FIONA      something in my middle flutters

JANE      what about work?
what will they say?
doesn't matter what they say, he says
i can't get up today
you go and tell them

FIONA      butterflies

LIZZIE      every now and again someone comes along with a
small cup of something thick and sweet that has a

taste of cough syrup
and when it doesn't come i cry
where are my children?
who has my children?
where are you taking me?
where is my man?
where is my man?
is he dead?
he must be dead

JANE          i run to the hotel
              run as fast as i can through the wet

FIONA         feet knocking against my ribcage

SALLY         sometimes i come home and he's curled up on the
              floor
              like a dog

JANE          i'm still wearing my slippers but it's too late to do
              anything about it
              what will i say?
              he is ill and can't come to work
              who will i say it to?
              i can't say it to the cook because She hates the
              head porter
              and i can't say it to the head porter because i can't
              go into the hall
              and i can't say it to the manager because He
              doesn't know i'm married to the coachman
              because He doesn't like that kind of thing and
              besides i'm wearing my slippers
              i wish i'd remembered to put on my hat
              people have only got so long to look at you so if
              you're wearing a hat that's all they've time to see

FIONA         there is something moving inside me

LIZZIE        God
              God

FIONA         was all the time spent trying and measuring and
              timetabling the heart out of what we were
              was that all for nothing?
              tell me

LIZZIE          i will be good, God
                i promise
                // cross my heart

JANE            // cross my heart
                it isn't the drink, i say
                he's ill, i say to the under porter
                well when will he be back? He says
                i'll have to tell Him upstairs
                that's what He'll want to know
                you know He sent one of the waiters packing last
                week and all he did was take a drink after hours
                your man had better watch it
                he'll be in tomorrow, i say
                i promise
                well he can't be that sick then, He says
                he's the under porter
                he's the Under Porter
                and now He's looking at me as if i owe him a
                favour
                he wants me to know that i'm below the lowest of
                the porters

SALLY           even when he hits me i can tell something has
                gone out of it for him

LIZZIE          i won't cry any more
                i promise

JANE            i look down in terrible anger
                God, let me be silent
                and i see my slippers
                my wet slippers
                and so does He
                i'll be in the kitchen every now and again, He says
                when the cook's not about
                i'll be expecting something extra from you

LIZZIE          no more drink, God
                no more pills
                no bad thing will pass my lips
                i swear

FIONA           i'm not surprised when the results come back

| | |
|---|---|
| SALLY | something has changed |
| LIZZIE | my children<br>if i could just see them |
| | // this once |
| JANE | // this once |
| FIONA | // this once |
| SALLY | // this once |
| FIONA | i promise I'll be good |
| SALLY | he says something<br>something that's almost // good |
| JANE | // good will come to the righteous |
| LIZZIE | because they have to be fed<br>and cared for |
| FIONA | i don't know how |
| SALLY | you think you're better than me, he says |
| | // i don't know |
| FIONA | // i don't |
| LIZZIE | i forget |
| JANE | i know you intend me for a purpose<br>and it isn't mine to question |
| LIZZIE | // but i don't want to stay here |
| SALLY | // but i don't want to stay here |
| FIONA | at first i'm keeping it as a surprise<br>and then it becomes a secret<br>a weird secret between me and the baby inside |
| LIZZIE | why does no one come to see me? |
| JANE | am i not good, God? |
| SALLY | you'll keep on with this work<br>won't you? he says |

JANE        // i don't know

LIZZIE      // i don't know

FIONA       there doesn't seem to be a right moment

SALLY       the way he says it
            he has no doubts

SALLY       // but i don't know

FIONA       // but i don't know

JANE        // but i don't know

LIZZIE      // but i don't know

JANE        how to improve our situation

FIONA       how to tell him

SALLY       how to leave

LIZZIE      where i am

FIONA       how to explain why i haven't told him before

JANE        where do i look for guidance?

FIONA       Jane Eyre would know the right thing to say

LIZZIE      a nurse brings me a small cup of something to
            calm me down
            but i'm calm enough
            i don't cry any more
            i understand that i'm being punished
            i don't know how long it'll last

FIONA       Jane Eyre was a plain speaker

SALLY       this life is hell

JANE        it's a struggle
            darning socks
            the yarn is thin and close-knit
            almost impossible to see with the naked eye

FIONA       but Jane Eyre isn't guided by passion
            maybe what i really need now is Anna Karenina

SALLY      i want to be free from this

JANE       i hold the sock away from me
           the hole is small
           i caught it early
           stitch in time, i hear my mother say
           and most of the sock is in good condition
           just the one wee hole

LIZZIE     there's a poor soul in the hospital garden
           he's very tall
           but bent over
           every now and again he stands to attention and
           turns his head as he watches something pass by
           i don't see what it is but i know it brings him to life
           one day he whispers to me

FIONA      Anna Karenina is filled with desperate longing

SALLY      so i rearrange the furniture
           and despise the fading carpet
           we need a new carpet

JANE       i hold the sock up to show him
           his father worked for a tailor
           so he appreciates a good stitch
           what do you think of that, Father?

LIZZIE     the tall bent gentleman has a soft voice
           i can hardly hear what he says at first

FIONA      Anna Karenina is tortured by her passions for a
           very long time

JANE       gggrggghhhhhhhh, he says

LIZZIE     i move a bit closer
           i'm sorry, i say
           could you say that again?

FIONA      *Middlemarch*
           George Eliot will get me through

SALLY      but now the curtains don't match
           they clash with the new carpet

FIONA      but George Eliot talks rings around me

JANE        he holds up his hand to signal stop

SALLY       did you hear?

JANE        i sit down on the edge of the chair

LIZZIE      what a lovely smile you have, says the captain
            that's what they all call him
            a lovely smile

SALLY       we
            need
            new
            curtains

FIONA       i'm pregnant, i say
            opting for Jane Eyre

SALLY       he makes a sudden move towards me and i jump
            back

FIONA       did you hear?

LIZZIE      i heard you that time, i say
            you said I have a lovely smile

JANE        gggggggggggrrrhhhhhhhhhhhh
            ghghghghghghghghghghghghgh
            uh
            uh
            uh

SALLY       HA, he shouts

LIZZIE      i smile at him and his face makes my smile back at
            me

FIONA       it's a surprise, i say

SALLY       BOO

LIZZIE      there isn't much to say out there in the garden
            but i feel very comfortable sitting on the seat
            beside him
            every now and again he turns and looks at me as
            though i've done something good
            and i feel good

FIONA      you are good, he says
           didn't you know that?

LIZZIE     // click

SALLY      // click

FIONA      // click

JANE       // click

           .

           .

           .

JANE       He's gone
           there He was
           and now He isn't

LIZZIE     where's my wee angel? i whisper to the captain

JANE       your father is in Heaven

SALLY      i have no good reason to stay

JANE       can He see us? the girls ask me

LIZZIE     why don't they let her visit?

FIONA      what if i can't love this child?

JANE       can He hear us? they ask

SALLY      the truth is

FIONA      i'm not ready

JANE       i listen

LIZZIE     she won't ever be coming, he says

JANE       i hear nothing

SALLY      // i am afraid of what comes next

FIONA      // i am afraid of what comes next

JANE       // i am afraid of what comes next

LIZZIE     // i am afraid of what comes next

JANE       i listen for His voice

LIZZIE      your wee angel rolled into the fire and died, he said
she's all dead now
all burned up and / dead

SALLY      gone

FIONA      i'm fit to pop

LIZZIE      my head cracks wide open and snakes come out of
it
i see them in his eyes
i put my hand up to touch them and they slither
over my wrist
i scream
the captain jumps up and salutes
someone comes with a harness and a needle
a needle and a harness

FIONA      i feel a tightening

LIZZIE      i don't feel anything

JANE      // nothing

FIONA      // nothing prepares me for this

SALLY      i can't take anything with me

FIONA      i suddenly think of the moment in *Anne of Green
Gables* when she knows the difference between
dreams and real life

SALLY      no photographs
nothing of a sentimental nature

LIZZIE      where is she?
what have they done with her?

JANE      i've come about the job, i say to the man at the
gates

FIONA      this is the hardest thing i've ever done

LIZZIE      come and look out the window, says the captain
past the chimneys
look
can you see her now?
can you see her?

| SALLY | i look at my daughter |
|---|---|
| LIZZIE | out in the fresh air<br>roses blooming in her cheeks<br>and her hair flying in the breeze |
| JANE | i've come about the job, i say<br>which job?<br>he says |
| SALLY | she asks if i'm coming back |
| FIONA | there are no books for this<br>i have no training for this |
| JANE | i can do any kind of job<br>i'm very hard-working |
| FIONA | i crawl back to bed and hide under the sheets<br>and pretend |
| LIZZIE | my wee angel girl has a dress with a petticoat<br>she has a doll and a pram that she pushes up and<br>down the harbour |
| FIONA | i think i've wet myself |
| SALLY | go go go |
| LIZZIE | is this true? |
| FIONA | my legs have locked<br>stuff pours out of me |
| LIZZIE | i have to get up<br>i have to move<br>i can't stay here<br>i have to go<br>i have to<br>// i have |
| JANE | // i have to work<br>take pity on our souls<br>i say<br>or my girls will be taken away from me |
| LIZZIE | i run and walk and walk and run and run and |

FIONA        wild horses couldn't stop me
             i have no control

SALLY        i don't know how far i get before i can't breathe
             i'm wet inside and out

JANE         the work in the city doesn't make sense

FIONA        do you mind if i sing? i ask the midwife.
             that's a first, she says

LIZZIE       where are you, angel?
             peekaboo

JANE         i know it isn't mine to question
             but
             why?

LIZZIE       huh
             huh
             huh
             huh
             huh
             huh
             huh
             huh

SALLY        huh
             huh
             huh
             huh
             huh
             huh
             huh
             huh

JANE         i listen for a voice

FIONA        aaaaaaaaaaaaaaaaaaaaaaaaaaaaaaaaaaaaaaaaaaaaaaaaa

JANE         i look for a sign

SALLY        huh
             huh
             huh
             huh

|          | huh<br>huh<br>huh<br>huh |
|----------|--------------------------|
| JANE     | Poor wee Jeanie, she's gettin awfy thin |
| LIZZIE   | wait for me<br>wait for me<br>wait for me, darlin |
| FIONA    | i'm the serpent<br>i'm bent and buckled |
| SALLY    | // keep going |
| JANE     | // keep going |
| FIONA    | OWWWWW |
| LIZZIE   | huhuh<br>huhuh<br>huhuh<br>huhuh |
| SALLY    | huh<br>huh<br>huh<br>huh |
| LIZZIE   | oh<br>oh<br>oh<br>oh<br>oh<br>oh<br>oh<br>oh |
| SALLY    | i'm nearly there |
| FIONA    | uhhhhhhhhhhhh – (*Post-childbirth euphoria.*) |
| LIZZIE   | you rest now, he says<br>forget, he says<br>you've not been well<br>he lies me down on the bed |

| | |
|---|---|
| SALLY | A muckle o bains covered ower wi skin |
| FIONA | she's perfect<br>she's curled up with her fist in her mouth<br>there's nothing i wouldn't do for her |
| SALLY | i should have gone a long time ago |
| LIZZIE | soon she'll be gettin a wee double chin |
| FIONA | i put my finger inside her little fist |
| JANE | // i'll always be here |
| LIZZIE | // i'll always be here |
| SALLY | // i'll always be here |
| FIONA | // i'll always be here |
| JANE | i won't forget |
| LIZZIE | i'll just have a sleep now |
| FIONA | and then waken up again<br>to traffic<br>birds<br>people on the stairs going to work<br><br>tick tock tick tock tick tock |
| LIZZIE | tick tock tick tock tick tock |
| SALLY | tick tock tick tock tick tock |
| JANE | tick tock tick tock tick tock |

# No BOOM

| | |
|---|---|
| HANNAH | Fae sookin Coulter's Candy |

*End.*

WHAT LOVE IS

Linda McLean

*For Blandine Pélissier and Sarah Vermande*

**Characters**

JEAN, *older woman*
GENE, *older man*
JEANETTE, *younger woman*

**Note on the Text**

*A double forward slash (//) indicates characters saying the
same thing at the same time.*

*A single forward slash (/) indicates interrupted speech.*

*What Love Is* was first performed at Òran Mór, Glasgow, as part
of 'A Play, a Pie and a Pint'on 4 April, 2011, with the following
cast:

| | |
|---|---|
| JEAN | Irene Macdougall |
| GENE | Peter Kelly |
| JEANETTE | Lesley Hart |
| *Director* | Emma Faulkner |

JEAN *and* GENE *dance into the room.*

*Tango.*

*With every turn of the head, they look towards the front door.*

*Or the window.*

*There's a noise from a phone.*

*They stop immediately and become unable to dance.*

*They watch the phone and the door and the window.*

*The phone stops.*

| | |
|---|---|
| GENE | Fuck |
| JEAN | Fuck fuck fuck fuck fuck |
| GENE | Fuck<br>Ffffffffffffffffffffffffffff |
| JEAN | Phone<br>Keys<br>Purse<br>That's your job, Gene |
| GENE | Only when I'm in the room, Jean<br>I can't remind her<br>If I'm not in the effing room |
| JEAN | Effing room? |
| GENE | Effing blinding room, Jean<br>Were you here?<br>Did you give her the kiss goodbye?<br>The cheery wave?<br>The 'don't hurry back on our account'? |

JEAN *nearly objects but hasn't the heart.*

Yes you were

| | |
|---|---|
| JEAN | I've never been called on to do the phone, keys, purse but |
| GENE | Phone keys purse but<br>Butt |

*Smacks her bum.*

| | |
|---|---|
| JEAN | Hey<br>Hey<br>That's my arse |
| GENE | Hey hey<br>That's my hand |
| JEAN | You must be forgetting that I'm a feminist |
| GENE | You must be forgetting that so am I |
| JEAN | ? |
| GENE | I gave you the fucking vote<br>Didn't I? |
| JEAN | So you did<br>That was nice<br>I must have caught you unawares |
| GENE | And where's my thanks? |
| JEAN | On the ballot paper<br>Every election<br>Everybody else is marking an X in case they can't spell their name<br>But I'm signing a kiss<br>Just for you. |

JEAN *puckers up and waits for a kiss.*

*She nearly gets it but the phone makes a noise again.*

*They spring back.*

*Door.*

*Window.*

*Phone stops.*

|          | Is it going to do that<br>Non-stop? |
|----------|-------------------------------------|
| GENE     | It probably is<br>It usually does<br>Doesn't it? |
| JEAN     | It's<br>Em<br>…<br>I find it |
| GENE     | A pain in the arse |
| JEAN     | Yes<br>Yes<br>Well<br>At any rate<br>Alarming |
| GENE     | I could fix it |
| JEAN     | To what extent? |
| GENE     | Extent?<br>What do you mean?<br>Is there a sliding scale of fixing? |
| JEAN     | I do believe there is |
| GENE     | Beginning where?<br>Ending when? |
| JEAN     | As with most manufactured goods<br>I imagine it extends all the way from<br>Dashing its brains out on the floor to<br>Technical wizardry<br>At which point along that spectrum did you<br>intend to create a fix? |
| GENE     | I could probably turn it off |
| JEAN     | My my |
| GENE     | Could you?<br>Could you? |

| | |
|---|---|
| JEAN | I think I could |
| GENE | You think you could? |
| JEAN | The on-off switch is always the easiest to locate |

*She makes a lightning-quick karate chop straight to his Adam's apple but barely touches him.*

*He chokes.*

*He can't breathe.*

*He doubles over.*

*She gives him a great big life-saving kiss.*

| | |
|---|---|
| GENE | You always take advantage |
| JEAN | You always underestimate me |
| GENE | …<br>I remember how you were |

*Oh no not that now.*
*Yes that.*
*Now.*

| | |
|---|---|
| JEAN | I remember how you were |
| GENE | Can you bear it? |
| JEAN | Some days better than others<br>Can you? |
| GENE | … |
| JEAN | Can you not? |
| GENE | The way things look<br>It's always been<br>…<br>If you asked me<br>Even then<br>I would have said<br>The way things look<br>Matters to me |

JEAN          Have I passed the point?

GENE          …

JEAN          You said you'd tell me
              You promised

GENE          You made me promise

JEAN          Have I passed the point?

              *He almost tells her his truth.*

              *He almost doubts himself.*

              *He almost forgets what she asked him.*

              *The phone makes its noise again.*

              *He dashes its brains out on the floor.*

              *She gasps and falls.*

GENE          What's wrong?
              Are you okay?
              What's wrong?

JEAN          Jesus mary and joseph jesus mary and joseph
              jesus mary and joseph jesus mary and

              GENE *signals her to stop with his hands.*

              *She looks around warily.*

              Did I
              What?
              Was I?
              ?

GENE          No
              No

JEAN          What then?

GENE          I'm a Catholic
              You know?
              Do you mind taking it just a wee bit easy with
              the jesus mary and joseph?

JEAN
…
Ha
I love the way you can still surprise me
…
I'm half Catholic

GENE
No you're not
You're not half anything

JEAN
Yes I am
Yes I am
YES I AM

GENE
Okay

JEAN
Take that back
Take that back

GENE
I take it back

JEAN
Take it back properly

GENE
I TAKE IT BACK

JEAN
You do?

GENE
Took it
Way back
Way back then
Took it back
It's took

JEAN
That's nice
You broke her phone

GENE
I hate that noise

JEAN
You could have changed it

GENE
Really?

JEAN
I think so

GENE
Have I ever done that?

JEAN
I'm not sure

*They consider the phone.*

*They consider the past.*

It was my fault

GENE    It was my fault

…

…

Now we don't know who's calling

JEAN    We wouldn't know anyway
Even if we saw their names
She doesn't tell us

GENE    Oh
Oh
Well
I know
I know
But
She's young
Younger
Generation
Nothing to

JEAN    I know you love her

GENE    No
Everything to
Em
Yes
Only live once

JEAN    Yes
Even now
(*Whispering*.) After everything

GENE    She doesn't
Can't
Know you know?
Can't
You can't
She can't
She doesn't know
Any
Bet[ter] different

| | |
|---|---|
| JEAN | But you'd think |
| GENE | No |
| JEAN | No? |
| GENE | No room for old thinking<br>No room for old |
| JEAN | … |
| GENE | I wasn't calling you old |
| JEAN | … |
| GENE | You look |
| JEAN | Don't say |
| GENE | // The same |
| JEAN | // The same |
| GENE | Same |
| JEAN | To you maybe |
| GENE | Enough<br>Same enough |
| JEAN | Enough?<br>I look the same enough?<br>Get me the mirror. |
| GENE | Get me the effing mirror? |
| JEAN | Get me the fucking mirror<br>Get it |

*In front of the mirror.*

I hate the mirror

| | |
|---|---|
| GENE | She loves the mirror |
| JEAN | The mirror loves her |
| GENE | Didn't we love her? |
| JEAN | We loved her |
| GENE | Enough? |

| | |
|---|---|
| JEAN | Too much? |
| GENE | Is that possible? |
| JEAN | Is that possible? |
| GENE | I don't know |
| JEAN | I don't know how a mirror works |
| GENE | Just light and dark |
| JEAN | Oh |
| GENE | Light and dark |
| JEAN | I used to be light |
| GENE | You have light |
| JEAN | Do I? |
| GENE | Look there<br>Look now<br>Light on your cheek<br>Your smiling cheek<br>Isn't that a smile I know?<br>I think it is |
| JEAN | She has my smile |
| GENE | Almost<br>She almost has your smile<br>But it stops<br>Just there<br>Just before it lights her eye |
| JEAN | I don't think that's my fault |
| GENE | You smiled at her<br>Plenty<br>You smiled at her when you could have been smiling at me |
| JEAN | She has your eyes<br>Every time I look at her<br>I see your eyes |

GENE    My eyes
        Your smile

        *And she smiles with her full smile and he*
        *looks with his beautiful eyes and it's almost as*
        *if we can see the other in the room.*

JEAN    She loves you
        That's for sure
        I should have known how it would be
        All those fairy tales
        All those beloved fathers
        And wicked mothers

GENE    Wicked stepmothers

JEAN    Dead mothers then
        Dead mothers is worse

GENE    She loves us both

JEAN    She does say so

GENE    She says it
        Often

JEAN    Do you ever doubt it?
        (*Whispers*.) Do you ever think she doesn't
        love you?

GENE    No
        Well
        You know how things are

JEAN    We can't know how things are
        How can we?

GENE    No
        No
        Things change

JEAN    Love?
        You think love changes?

GENE    It used to mean something else
        Maybe we don't know what love means now

| | |
|---|---|
| JEAN | Of course |
| | Of course that's what it is |
| | We don't know what love means now |
| | Old thinking |
| | We're old thinking |
| | We can't say love |
| | And mean the |
| | The same love |
| | That's |
| | For sure |
| | That's what it is |
| | Oh I'm so pleased |
| GENE | Well |
| | Pleased? |
| | Well now |
| | I'm a bit confused |
| JEAN | That's okay |
| | It's [day of the week] |
| GENE | I effing know what day it is |
| JEAN | Effing know? |
| GENE | I effing do |
| JEAN | Okay |
| | If you say so |
| GENE | It's effing [day of the week] |
| JEAN | Should I remind you that I just said that? |
| | A minute ago |
| GENE | I effing know that |
| | Too |
| JEAN | Because you were confused |
| GENE | No |
| | Confused? |
| | I don't think so |
| | No |
| | … |
| | ? |

| | |
|---|---|
| JEAN | You don't remember what we were talking about<br>It's all right<br>I don't remember either |
| GENE | I don't remember |
| JEAN | No<br>It's easy to lose track now<br>Isn't it? |
| GENE | Well there we have a meeting of minds |
| JEAN | Just there? |
| GENE | No<br>No<br>No maybe<br>Did she say when she was coming back? |
| JEAN | Could be late<br>Don't wait up she says<br>Kiss on the forehead<br>Flick on the cheek |
| GENE | But not definite |
| JEAN | Is she ever definite? |
| GENE | Yes<br>Oh yes<br>I'm pretty sure<br>…<br>No |
| JEAN | No |
| GENE | She never says no |
| JEAN | Or yes |
| GENE | Maybe |
| JEAN | Maybe<br>That's what she says<br>I may be late<br>I may have a horrible night and come home early |

|  |  |
|---|---|
|  | Don't make any plans<br>She's definite about that |
| GENE | And shortbread |
| JEAN | Yes<br>YES |
| GENE | She's very definite about shortbread |
| JEAN | Always loved shortbread |
| GENE | Shortbread always cheers her up |
| JEAN | Have you made it? |
| GENE | Well I don't make the shortbread |
| JEAN | Yes<br>Today<br>Yes |
| GENE | No<br>I do phone keys purse |
| JEAN | Not today<br>Today you were doing shortbread<br>You were adding<br>A little something? |
| GENE | Well<br>Yes<br>Was I? |
| JEAN | A little<br>A-mi-trip-tyline? |
| GENE | Was I?<br>Oh<br>Well |
| JEAN | Did you change your mind? |
| GENE | I<br>I |
| JEAN | I'd like to know if you changed your mind |
| GENE | I don't remember |

| | |
|---|---|
| JEAN | Oh<br>Oh |
| GENE | But now I feel sad<br>I feel very sad<br>When I think of shortbread |
| JEAN | Yes?<br>So you made it then?<br><br>*Door.*<br><br>*Window.* |
| GENE | Do you think we'll ever go home? |
| JEAN | This is our home |
| GENE | But do you think we'll ever go there? |
| JEAN | Silly |
| GENE | Jean? |
| JEAN | Don't be silly |
| GENE | You know what I mean |
| JEAN | Tt<br>Shh<br>Anyone<br>(*Whisper.*) Anyone listening<br>Would think you were silly<br>Very silly<br>They might start to think that you were in need of<br>…<br>Medication |
| GENE | I take my medication<br>What's wrong with that?<br>My medication helps me sleep |
| JEAN | Other medication<br>The kind that makes the floor tilt<br>Or<br>Or<br>Worse |

GENE            Yes but
                You know I'm not in need of anything like that

JEAN            Yes but
                I don't make those decisions
                Do I?

GENE            I was only saying to you
                Here
                In private

                *She looks round.*

                *And smiles.*

                *She smiles meaningfully at him.*

                *They look round.*

                *And up.*

                *They smile as if at cameras.*

JEAN            I sometimes have the feeling it's never private

                *They sway towards each other.*

                *Some fragments of tango.*

                Besides
                It's much nicer now
                We have new windows
                And
                And
                Em
                Things
                Cushions
                Fabrics
                Everything
                Much more
                Well look how up to date we are

GENE            Up to date?

JEAN            Tut
                Don't you remember how
                Floral
                We were?

|       | Heavens<br>We were<br>Good Lord<br>Laura Ashleyfied<br>Jeez |
|-------|---|
| GENE  | Steady on |
| JEAN  | Well<br>You know<br>Our furnishings<br>Our fabrics<br>were not<br>Thought<br>Through |
| GENE  | Really? |
| JEAN  | Don't you remember how<br>Rest-ful<br>It felt<br>When we came back and saw how it had changed? |
| GENE  | I didn't notice<br>I was just so glad to have you back |
| JEAN  | Yes<br>She did a lovely job<br>Didn't she? |
| GENE  | I didn't notice |
| JEAN  | But you notice now |
| GENE  | It just all looks so |
| JEAN  | Neutral |
| GENE  | Unfamiliar |
| JEAN  | Restful |

*They couldn't be more distant from one another.*

*They couldn't be more together.*

| GENE  | You were on a machine |

JEAN   Now now

GENE   The machine was blowing breath into you

JEAN   I think that's a dream

GENE   No
      I saw it
      POOFFF
      SHHUHH
      POOFF
      SHHUHH
      POOFFF

JEAN   My dream
      I think it's my dream

GENE   SHHUHH

JEAN   I'm seven years old and an aeroplane flies
      over my head

GENE   POOFFF

JEAN   Really high
      So high it leaves a trail
      A jet
      It's a jet
      I don't know that at the time
      But that's what it is

GENE   SHHUHH

JEAN   But I know it's going far

GENE   POOFFF
      SHHUHH
      POOFFF
      SHUHHH

JEAN   Shh
      It isn't the dream where I die
      That comes later
      This is the dream where I see the plane and
      see myself on the plane and see myself as
      seven and seventy at the same time and know
      it isn't too late

| | |
|---|---|
| GENE | POOFFFF |
| JEAN | And SNAP<br>SNAP |
| GENE | You snapped right out of it |
| JEAN | Snapped right out of it<br>Wide awake |
| GENE | I was there |
| JEAN | You were there |
| GENE | Your eyes snapped wide open |
| JEAN | And I said 'it isn't too late'<br>'We can still go'<br>'The world still belongs to us'<br>'We can do whatever we want' |
| GENE | You said<br>Wahr wahr wahr wahrr<br>Uuuhh<br>With your mouth twisted |
| JEAN | You didn't understand me |
| GENE | You said<br>Wahr wahr wahr<br>Not to mention the dribble<br>And your tongue on the outside of your mouth<br>Instead of the inside |
| JEAN | I thought you would understand |
| GENE | Even if it was now<br>Even if it was tomorrow<br>And you fell over<br>And woke up<br>And said<br>Wahr wahr whar<br>I wouldn't understand you |
| JEAN | If I fell over tomorrow<br>And then woke up<br>I wouldn't say 'it isn't too late' |

| | |
|---|---|
| GENE | You see?<br>How am I supposed to keep up? |
| JEAN | When did that happen? |
| GENE | Two three years<br>Five?<br>More? |
| JEAN | I mean<br>When did you stop understanding me? |
| GENE | I've never understood wahr wahr wahr |
| JEAN | But you've said<br>We've said<br>So many times I can't remember<br>We've said things at exactly the same time<br>On the same thought<br>Same breath<br>One heart<br>One mind |
| GENE | Oh |
| JEAN | Oh |
| GENE | Well not wahr wahr<br>Wahr<br>I've never had that thought |
| JEAN | It'll come to you<br>One day |
| GENE | And you'll understand what I mean by that?<br>Will you? |
| JEAN | I don't know |
| GENE | You won't understand |
| JEAN | I like to think if you were looking at me with<br>a dream in your face<br>In your eyes<br>In the sudden snapping-on of the lights<br>I like to think I would understand something<br>Of what you meant |

| | |
|---|---|
| GENE | I thought you were hungry |
| JEAN | You<br>Were hungry |
| GENE | You hadn't had a proper meal in weeks<br>Was it weeks or months? |
| JEAN | You<br>Hadn't had a proper meal<br>I wasn't hungry<br>They had me on a drip |
| GENE | You've always been so fond of your food<br>Such a keen sense of taste<br>And bite<br>I was sure you must have been missing it<br>I took one look at the sudden snap<br>And saw<br>Fillet steak with roast potatoes and oven-roasted vegetables<br>And Yorkshire pudding |
| JEAN | I don't like Yorkshire pudding |
| GENE | I make lovely Yorkshire pudding |
| JEAN | I know you do |
| GENE | And gravy<br>Home-made |
| JEAN | Home-made |
| GENE | Good gravy<br>Oh yes<br>Oh<br>Oh |
| JEAN | What? |
| GENE | I haven't made Yorkshire pudding |
| JEAN | No<br>No |

GENE

I
Oh
When was the last time?
Oh
I know
He came round
It was
Yes I think I've nearly got it
He came to our house
The one that used to be here
He came
Was that
Was that the last

JEAN

Don't fret yourself

GENE

WAS THAT THE LAST YORKSHIRE
PUDDING?
Have I not made a Yorkshire pudding since

JEAN

You did
You have
Everybody loved it
You made them in heart-shaped tins

GENE

Oh yes
Bloody awkward tins

JEAN

You love a challenge

GENE

Valentine's day

JEAN

Valentine's day

GENE

They rose
So high
I worried about the highness

JEAN

They were perfect
Your pastry has always been perfect
Full of
Love
And lightness

GENE

You don't like Yorkshire pudding

| JEAN | If I had to eat Yorkshire pudding<br>Yours would be the only one |
|---|---|
| GENE | …<br>I didn't make it for you |
| JEAN | I know |
| GENE | I didn't make it for her |
| JEAN | No |
| GENE | We lost him<br>Didn't we? |
| JEAN | Not our fault |
| GENE | Not<br>Our<br>Fault |

*Door.*

*Window.*

…

*Door.*

*They listen for something.*

*Maybe a click.*

*Maybe a stockinged foot on the stairs.*

*Maybe nothing but they nod to each other and close their eyes standing up.*

*The door inches open.*

*A lovely young woman, JEANETTE, comes quietly into the space.*

*She tiptoes over to JEAN.*

| JEANETTE | Are you asleep? |
|---|---|

*JEAN exaggerates an open-eyed wink.*

I knew you'd be up

| | |
|---|---|
| JEAN | Shh |
| JEANETTE | He sleeps a lot now, doesn't he? |
| JEAN | He was always a bit of a slug |

GENE *exaggerates an open eye.*

| | |
|---|---|
| JEANETTE | I knew you weren't sleeping |
| GENE | No you didn't |
| JEANETTE | Course I did |
| GENE | How then?<br>How? |
| JEANETTE | I always know |
| GENE | No you don't |
| JEANETTE | Oh yes I do |
| GENE | No<br>You only think that |

GENE *shouldn't continue with this.*

| | |
|---|---|
| | Sometimes I'm not sleeping and you don't know |
| JEANETTE | I always know |
| GENE | Well are you pretending then? |
| JEANETTE | Are you?<br>Do you pretend you're sleeping to me?<br>Why would you do that? |

*Oops.*

| | |
|---|---|
| GENE | I<br>Don't<br>Know |
| JEAN | He forgets |
| GENE | I just want to know how she knows |
| JEANETTE | I have young ears |

| | |
|---|---|
| GENE | Oh |
| JEANETTE | And young eyes |
| GENE | Oh yes<br>My eyes |
| JEANETTE | And I've been watching the two of you since I was born so I know you better than you do |
| GENE | I spy |
| JEANETTE | What? |
| GENE | I SPY<br>With my little eye |
| JEANETTE | …? |
| GENE | Something beginning with |
| JEANETTE | …? |
| GENE | Something beginning with J |
| JEANETTE | …? |
| GENE | Jeanette, silly. |

GENE *looks at* JEAN.

| | |
|---|---|
| JEANETTE | What have you two been up to? |
| JEAN | // Nothing |
| GENE | // Nothing |
| JEANETTE | Oh<br>Oh oh oh<br>What have you two been up to? |

JEANETTE *looks briefly at* JEAN *but then circles on* GENE.

*He's flustered.*

Do think I'm stupid?
Do you think I don't know when something's been going on here?

*He looks briefly at something to do with the broken phone.*

*Her eye follows his.*

*She strolls over and picks the bits up.*

*They hold their breath.*

*Door.*

*Window.*

I can't leave you alone for a minute
Can I?
What am I going to do with you?
Hm?
If you can't be trusted
What do I do then?
I'm supposed to be able to leave you alone
Do you know what happens if I can't trust
you for half an hour?
I don't know
I don't know what to do with you

*They've stopped breathing.*

What are you like?

*They don't know.*

*But they breathe again, just.*

Children
You're like children

*They know they're not children.*

*But they don't know what to do.*

GENE            Children are wonderful

JEANETTE        I'm sure they are

GENE            Oh yes they are
                Oh yes
                If you ever get the chance
                You must have one
                More than one
                Just in case
                You know?

JEAN          Gene
              Gene

GENE          Oh don't tell me you don't remember?
              What fun
              Oh yes
              Hard work but what fun
              Swinging
              And lifting
              And monsters on the floor
              And oh the stories

JEAN          Stop now

GENE          But if we don't encourage her
              If we don't put the idea in her head
              She might not have any
              How sad would that be?
              So sad

JEANETTE      And where will I get the time?
              Tell me that?
              I go to work
              I come home
              I make your food
              I make your beds
              I change you when you don't get to the toilet
              in time

JEAN          Please

GENE          What?
              What?
              Don't be silly
              What?
              No
              You're getting confused
              We change you
              We feed you
              We go to work
              We're the ones

JEAN          Not any more

GENE
Yes
We go to work
I'm a
You go to work
You're a
A
A
ehh
I'm a
I'm a
An engineer
I'm an engineer
'Where's my gear
I'm an engineer
Here's your gear
Mister Engineer'

JEAN *looks at* JEANETTE.

JEANETTE *considers that look.*

JEANETTE
I hope we're not going to have a discussion now
Are we?
Were you intending to follow that look up in some way?
Because I'm on my way back out
I had a horrible feeling I left something here
Not the phone
I don't care about the phone
Something else I couldn't quite put my finger on
But it nagged at me
And nagged at me
Until I had to come back
Maybe I was worried
Do you think that might be it?
Was I worried about something?

JEAN
I don't know darling
Were you?

JEANETTE
Is there something I should be worried about?

JEAN             I don't think so darling

JEANETTE         Darling?
                 Hmm
                 Hmm

GENE             Are you all right?
                 You two?
                 Is everything all right?

JEANETTE         She just called me darling
                 Twice
                 What do you think about that?

GENE             Oh I love it when she calls me darling

JEANETTE         Hmm

GENE             Oh yes

JEANETTE         When does she call you darling?

GENE             Em
                 'Gene darling
                 Would you like a coffee?'
                 That's one
                 And
                 Em
                 'Gene darling
                 Em
                 'Gene darling
                 Could we have the volume down?'
                 That's
                 That's another
                 Em

JEANETTE         But what does it mean
                 When she says that?
                 What does it mean?

GENE             It means
                 Well the first one
                 'Would you like a coffee?'
                 Usually means
                 Would I like to make a coffee for her?

| | |
|---|---|
| JEANETTE | Ha<br>Exactly<br>It means<br>Will you make HER a coffee |
| GENE | Yes but nicer than that<br>I don't mind<br>Sometimes I say no<br>'No I wouldn't like a coffee' |
| JEAN | But you make it anyway |
| JEANETTE | And 'can we have the volume down?' |
| GENE | Means<br>Will I turn down the volume on the telly<br>Or the radio |
| JEANETTE | See<br>So<br>Gene, darling<br>Darling<br>Means she wants something |
| GENE | Well |
| JEANETTE | Oh come on<br>Don't be silly<br>I'm right<br>Aren't I? |
| GENE | Well |
| JEANETTE | Of course I am<br>I'm right |
| JEAN | Yes<br>Yes<br>You're right |
| JEANETTE | Ha<br>I knew it |
| JEAN | Yes<br>You know us too well |
| JEANETTE | So? |

JEAN        Yes

JEANETTE    What did you want?

JEAN        Nothing

JEANETTE    No no no no no

JEAN        Nothing for myself

JEANETTE    Hmmm
            What then?

JEAN        I was going to ask you to be kind to him

            *Woooooo.*

            *That's a bit dangerous.*

JEANETTE    Emmmmmm

            JEANETTE *is agitated by this.*

            *Her foot or leg or some limb taps away as if it's gnawing at that last statement.*

            Mmmmmmmmmmm

JEAN        He hasn't been rhyming like that for a long time
            It isn't usual
            These days

JEANETTE    Something wrong
            Something wrong there
            Something
            Yes
            Yes
            No
            You
            You
            You told a lie
            You told me a lie
            It's for you
            It's always for you
            You meant
            You want me to be nice to you

|  | It's what you always want<br>It's like there's a bottomless nice-to-you pit<br>And I am nice to you |
|---|---|
| GENE | Yes<br>You're very good to us darling<br>I mean |
| JEANETTE | Shh |
| GENE | You look after us |
| JEANETTE | Be quiet<br>Or I'll forget<br>You can't keep a straight train of thought in<br>your head |
| GENE | Yes I can |
| JEANETTE | Why do you think I'm not nice to you? |
| JEAN | I didn't say that |
| JEANETTE | No<br>No<br>Never saying it<br>Just the look<br>Just the<br>No<br>No<br>I can't have this discussion now<br>Why do you always want me to TALK about<br>things?<br>I was worried<br>Why was I worried?<br>I don't know<br>An instinct<br>A fear<br>For you<br>For one of you |
| JEAN | You don't have to worry about us |
| JEANETTE | Of course I do<br>I can't leave you alone for a half-hour stretch |

|  | but something happens<br>Something untoward |
| --- | --- |
| JEAN | Nothing happened<br>Nothing untoward happened |
| GENE | She fell over |
| JEAN | Not really |
| GENE | She fell down |
| JEANETTE | Tonight?<br>You fell over tonight? |
| JEAN | No<br>He means before<br>When I had the stroke |
| JEANETTE | Did she fall over tonight?<br>Tell me<br>I knew I was worried about something |
| GENE | Yes<br>Yes |
| JEANETTE | When?<br>How? |
| GENE | Just after I<br>Or before the<br>When the phone |
| JEAN | The phone fell<br>It was the phone that fell |
| JEANETTE | You fell<br>You fell |
| JEAN | It wasn't really a fall |
| JEANETTE | Why do you want to hide it from me? |
| JEAN | Because it wasn't a fall<br>It was a |
| JEANETTE | Fall |

| | |
|---|---|
| JEAN | Stumble<br>Not the kind of fall you think<br>Not the kind that everybody says<br>'Oh she fell<br>Oh that'll be the start of it<br>One break<br>After that first break they're never right again'<br>It wasn't that kind of fall |
| JEANETTE | A fall nonetheless |
| JEAN | Nothing's broken |
| JEANETTE | Apart from my phone |
| JEAN | I didn't break your |
| JEANETTE | No?<br>You didn't break my phone?<br>How is it broken then? |
| GENE | It was my fault<br>It's all my fault<br>Isn't it?<br>I can tell |
| JEAN | No<br>It isn't<br>It wasn't<br>It was mine |
| JEANETTE | Uhhhhhh |
| GENE | What?<br>What is it? |
| JEANETTE | You two<br>I'm just so weary |

*She sits down and takes off her shoes.*

*Window.*

*Door.*

| | |
|---|---|
| GENE | Are you staying in then?<br>Staying in? |

| | |
|---|---|
| JEANETTE | I don't have the energy to go back out |
| GENE | Won't<br>You know<br>Anybody<br>Be expecting you? |
| JEANETTE | I'm always expected |
| GENE | Oh<br>Oh |

*GENE and JEAN don't want her to stay in.*

*Smallest fragments of tango in their gestures.*

| | |
|---|---|
| JEANETTE | What are you doing? |
| GENE | Nothing |
| JEAN | Nothing |
| JEANETTE | I know that<br>But you're fidgeting<br>Or something<br>Just<br>Be still<br>For heaven's sake |

*They try to be still.*

*GENE has a small nervous gesture.*

*JEAN takes his hand.*

*They stand face to face.*

*GENE smiles at JEAN.*

*She smiles right back at him.*

*She keeps hold of his hand but moves to stand beside him.*

*He closes his eyes.*

*When he opens them he doesn't remember what just happened.*

| | |
|---|---|
| GENE | Oh you're there |

| JEANETTE | Yes I'm here |
| GENE | Would you like a cup of tea? |
| JEANETTE | I don't know |
| GENE | Oh go on |
| JEANETTE | I don't know<br>I don't know if I'm staying in |
| JEAN | She doesn't want a cup of tea |
| JEANETTE | I didn't say that |
| GENE | I can see if there's any shortbread |
| JEANETTE | Did you make shortbread? |
| JEAN | No<br>I didn't make any |
| JEANETTE | Oh<br>You usually make shortbread |
| JEAN | I didn't<br>Today |
| GENE | I feel sad whenever I think of shortbread |
| JEANETTE | Me too<br>But only when there isn't any |
| JEAN | I didn't make any |
| JEANETTE | Tt<br>I could murder a piece of shortbread<br>Shortbread makes me feel<br>Hopeful<br>You know?<br>You know<br>I don't know what's wrong<br>I don't know why I came back<br>Maybe I wasn't worried about you<br>Maybe the thing that was nagging at me<br>Was me<br>Maybe I was fed up with going out to the<br>same places |

With the same people
Even when they're not the same people
They are
The same kind of people
Hearing the same stories
Moans
Complaints
Dreams that never come true
Love that never happens
Love that seems to be an old dream
A fantasy
Maybe the thing that was nagging at me
Was
…
…

JEAN            What?
                What was really nagging at you?

JEANETTE        …
                Oh I don't know
                Nothing
                It was probably nothing

JEAN            No
                Something was nagging at you
                What was it?

JEANETTE        I
                I
                I

JEAN            Change
                Was it change that was nagging at you?

JEANETTE        You say the daftest things
                Change?
                What kind of change?

JEAN            Change from this
                Change from us

GENE            What do you mean?
                Jean

| | |
|---|---|
| JEANETTE | I don't want a change from you |
| JEAN | Yes<br>Yes<br>You want to fly off<br>You want to<br>See<br>Floating islands in a lake high up in the Andes<br>The buried people in Pompeii<br>The aurora borealis<br>The<br>The<br>The<br>Rhinoceroses<br>And<br>Flocks of sea eagles in<br>In<br>Thailand |
| JEANETTE | Huh |
| GENE | Are you going to leave? |
| JEAN | Yes |
| JEANETTE | No |
| GENE | Is she going to leave? |
| JEAN | Yes<br>Yes<br>She wants to<br>You want to |
| JEANETTE | Well of course I want to<br>Who wouldn't want to? |
| JEAN | You can<br>You<br>Can |
| JEANETTE | Ha |
| JEAN | Don't let it get too late |
| JEANETTE | Where to start<br>I wouldn't even know where to |

GENE        But I don't want you to go
            I don't want her to go

JEAN        It's all right

GENE        But what will I do?

JEAN        You'll have me

GENE        It's not the same
            It's not the same

JEAN        Please
            Please
            We're just talking
            She's isn't going anywhere right now
            She's right here

JEANETTE    How can I go anywhere?

            *Door. Window.*

            JEANETTE *stands up and leaves the room.*

GENE        Is she going?
            Where is she going?

JEAN        Not far

GENE        What if she does go far?
            What if she doesn't come back?

JEAN        Her shoes are still here
            See.

            *The shoes.*

            *Hmmm.*

            *Those shoes are really something.*

            *High-status shoes, platforms.*

            *Big fuck-off platforms.*

            *And shiny.*

GENE        She left her shoes

JEAN        She left her shoes

| | |
|---|---|
| GENE | What does it mean? |
| JEAN | It means she must be coming back |
| GENE | Does it? |
| JEAN | She loves those shoes |
| GENE | How does she walk in them? |
| JEAN | Don't be silly<br>We've all worn high shoes |
| GENE | Not me |
| JEAN | Even you wore platforms, Gene |
| GENE | Ha |
| JEAN | I thought you were four inches taller than you really were |
| GENE | Jean Genie<br>Lives on his back<br>Jean Genie<br>Da da da da<br>Jean Genie<br>Let yourself go<br>Wo woh<br>Dun duh ruh<br>Dun duh nuh duh |
| JEAN | Or it could mean that she's gone to bed |
| GENE | She was weary |
| JEAN | And fed up |
| GENE | Yes<br>You made her fed up |
| JEAN | No<br>Don't say that |
| GENE | Has she left her shoes before? |
| JEAN | …<br>… |

*The shoes have become a wee bit sinister now.*

GENE *circles on them.*

GENE    She's never left them before

JEAN    Please leave them alone

*GENE steps into the shoes.*

*He's taller.*

*And straighter.*

GENE    'You
What are you like?
You're like children'

*Oooooo.*

JEAN    Stop now

GENE    'I can't leave you for a minute
I'm supposed to be able to leave you for a
minute'

JEAN    If she catches you in those shoes

GENE    'Something is nagging at me
What's nagging at me?
Why am I worried?
Why am I not happy?
Everyone expects me
When do I have time?
Is there no tea?
Is there no shortbread?'

*Door.*

*Window.*

I don't feel ha / ppy [when I think of
shortbread]

JEAN    I know.

*He forgets he's wearing the shoes and tries to
walk normally.*

*His feet get a bit mixed up.*

*That's a bit of a surprise to him.*

| | |
|---|---|
| GENE | Well how on earth did they get there? |
| JEAN | She left them |
| GENE | Where is she? |

*He doesn't take the shoes off.*

*They're a bit funny now.*

*He has some fun with them.*

*At some point in the next section he takes off the shoes.*

| | |
|---|---|
| JEAN | Would you like to go? |
| GENE | No<br>Where? |
| JEAN | Somewhere |
| GENE | Well where? |
| JEAN | Just not here any more |
| GENE | Home you mean? |
| JEAN | No<br>Away |
| GENE | Do we have money? |
| JEAN | Yes I think we do |
| GENE | Would we go there by bus? |
| JEAN | I don't know |
| GENE | Or boat? |
| JEAN | I really don't know |
| GENE | Or plane? |
| JEAN | I<br>I don't know |

GENE          Well Jean
              I think I need to hear a better plan
              Before I agree to it

JEAN          Ha

              …
              I love that you can still surprise me

GENE          I love it when I make you smile

              *They smile.*

JEAN          I love it when I make you smile

              JEAN *takes* GENE*'s hand and goes over to
              the window.*

              *She leans out.*

GENE          Is it cold?

JEAN          Not so bad

GENE          Dark but?

JEAN          Only at night-time

GENE          Hmmm

JEAN          It isn't too late

GENE          What if she doesn't come back?
              What then?

JEAN          That'll be all right

GENE          Will it?

JEAN          We'll be all right

GENE          What if something has happened to her?

JEAN          She's a big girl

GENE          Yes but / what if

JEAN          Do you want to go and look for her?
              Is that it?

GENE          Or you could?

| | |
|---|---|
| JEAN | You'd like me to go and look for her? |
| GENE | Yes<br>Yes<br>No<br>No I'll go |
| JEAN | Okay<br>You go then |

*Maybe this is when he steps out of the shoes.*

GENE *goes out.*

JEAN *has a moment with the shoes.*

*She doesn't know quite what to make of them.*

*Maybe something with her hands.*

*She has a funny feeling.*

*Something happens to her.*

*She sits on the floor.*

*Very still.*

*She isn't dead.*

*The thing that's happening is a bit like a strong wave.*

*She breathes to the rhythm of it.*

GENE *comes in.*

*He's carrying something.*

GENE    I've got a surprise for you
Jean
Shortbread
Sitting on the kitchen table
Look
Untouched
Virgin shortbread
Jean
Jean

|      | Don't be daft<br>Jean<br>Jean |
|------|-------------------------------|

.

.

.

| GENE | Oh<br>Oh<br>JEANETTE<br>JEANETTE<br>JEANETTE |
|------|-----------------------------------------------|
| JEAN | Wahr wahr wahr wahr |
| GENE | Don't say that |
| JEAN | Wahr wahr wahr wahr<br>Uhhhhhhhh |
| GENE | Don't do that Jean<br>Please<br>Don't do that |
| JEAN | WAHR WAHR WAHR WAHR WAHR |
| GENE | Oh Jean<br>Your tongue<br>Ooff<br>I don't like it<br>I don't like seeing you like that |

*She tries to make him understand something.*

*He doesn't.*

*He sits beside her.*

*He can't look at her.*

| GENE | Where is she? |
|------|---------------|
| JEAN | (*A lisping shhh.*) |
| GENE | Will we be all right? |

JEAN *can move one arm.*

*She grabs his hand.*

She'll be upset if she comes back and finds
this
She'll be angry with me
Why will she be angry with me?
There's no need for that
Being angry
No need
We were never angry with her
Well you wouldn't let us be angry with her
Would you?
You grew up with angry, you said
You didn't want it for her
Or him
Aw
Aw
Aw
We lost him didn't we?
Awwwww
Not our fault

*As he's talking, he absentmindedly takes a
piece of shortbread.*

JEAN        WAHR
               WAHR

GENE       I'm never going to understand wahr wahr
wahr Jean.
I'm sorry
I don't know if you want us to go in an
aeroplane
Or a boat
Or a bus
Or if you want a roast-beef dinner with oven-
roasted vegetables
And Yorkshire pudding

JEAN        Waaaaahhhrrrr

GENE       No Yorkshire pudding then

*She laughs an odd twisted-mouth laugh.*

Did I get that right?
No Yorkshire pudding

*He looks at her.*

*He uses his sleeve to wipe some moisture
away from her chin.*

*He looks in her eyes.*

*She snaps them wide open.*

Well how about a wee bit of shortbread then?

*She smiles a broad twisted smile.*

*She leans towards him in a way he knows.*

See?
See?
Same thought
Same breath
One heart
One mind

*He feeds her some shortbread.*

*He eats some himself.*

*They have a last tango, however that may be,
maybe just heads.*

*Door.*

*Window.*

**A Nick Hern Book**

*Sex & God* and *What Love Is* first published in Great Britain as a paperback original in 2012 by Nick Hern Books Limited, The Glasshouse, 49a Goldhawk Road, London W12 8QP, in association with Magnetic North Theatre Productions

Cover image by Fogbank Projects (www.fogbank.co.uk)
Cover designed by Ned Hoste, 2H

Typeset by Nick Hern Books, London
Printed in Great Britain by Mimeo Ltd, Huntingdon, Cambridgeshire PE29 6XX

A CIP catalogue record for this book is available from the British Library

ISBN    978 1 84842 300 8